A Salmon Fisher Remembers

A Salmon Fisher Remembers

Michael Forsyth-Grant

The Pentland Press
Edinburgh – Cambridge – Durham – USA

© Michael Forsyth-Grant, 1995

First published in 1995 by
The Pentland Press Ltd
1 Hutton Close,
South Church
Bishop Auckland
Durham

All rights reserved
Unauthorised duplication
contravenes existing laws

ISBN 1-85821-309-6

Typeset by Carnegie Publishing, 18 Maynard St, Preston
Printed and bound by Antony Rowe Ltd, Chippenham

*To Donald McIntyre and Ian McCreadie Smith
(both deceased) whose courage and zeal in two Drift Net
Wars greatly contributed to ultimate victory*

Contents

	Illustrations	ix
1	Genesis	1
2	A Military School	6
3	High Jinks in Edinburgh	12
4	An Apprentice Starts	17
5	The Rudiments of Sea-Salmon Fishing in 1939	21
6	The 1939 Salmon Season Opens	30
7	Sea-Salmon Fishing, 1939	39
8	An Apprentice in the Making	48
9	Salmon Fishers in Wartime	53
10	Ascending the Salmon Fisher's Ladder	60
11	The Golden Age of Scottish Salmon	71
12	Lapses of Security	79
13	The First Drift Net War	88
14	Some Angling Feats and Misadventures	102
15	The Second Drift War	115
16	The Last Years	128

Illustrations

Fishing a fly net.	22
Ashore with the fly net catch.	23
Fishing a fly net. George Thomson, salmon fisher first class, at Rossie station, Montrose, 1958.	24
Fishing a bag net in Lunan Bay, 1949.	27
Salmon transportation: pannier pony on Woodston cliff path.	28
River netting on the North Esk.	31
Planting a fly net. George Easton and a Ferguson post hole digger.	65
The railway bridge at Montrose.	67
Memorial to bygone prosperity: Montrose town hall.	72
Salmon angling: the author in the 1970s.	105
Charlie Valentine at the pondage pool.	107
James Harrington's red-letter day: 11 salmon in 3 hours.	108
Bill Gilbert.	108
Ken Adam: a very celebrated game-keeper and ghillie.	111
The war at sea: speedboat *Trafalgar*.	116
Police confiscating nets: second Drift Net War.	121
The war in the air: search and reconnaissance aircraft.	123

I

Genesis

The village of St Cyrus stands above the high cliffs in the centre of Montrose Bay, and at the top of the path leading from the village to the sands below there is a superb panoramic view. Milton Ness and Scurdiness are the sentinels which command the limits of the Bay that has a magnificent stretch of sands from St Cyrus to Montrose, which is a distance of some five miles.

Up to the end of the Second World War, and for two or three centuries before, St Cyrus was a busy rural hamlet dominated by two industries, farming and commercial salmon fishing, and the two were very interchangeable as the peak demands for labour between them occurred at different periods of the year. During the first half of this century, Montrose Bay was the most heavily netted and the most productive area for salmon of any part of the British Isles.

My family had lived in St Cyrus for generations, and farming and the sea was very much in our blood. From the age of four, when I was not playing about in the fields and woods, I was down on the sands, building castles and catching shrimps in the pools where the sands finally merged into rocks at the north-east corner of the Bay. Our family had a small wooden beach hut which was the HQ of the older generation, who sat in deck-chairs observing the antics of their offspring and, in summer, the constant comings and goings of the hordes of salmon fishers busy in their boats or climbing along the flynets. The cliffs are nearly 300 feet high, and the salmon had to be transported up the narrow bridle-path to the collecting depot at the top; for generations this had been done by a donkey with side panniers. The lad who led the donkey up and down the cliffs was aged about twelve – two years older than me. How I envied George Pittendreich and his job, and wished it could be mine!

Although George and I were great friends and often swapped yarns together while I admired the silvery salmon in the panniers, my ambition was not fulfilled. I was packed off to school in far-away Herefordshire, but salmon and fishing were never far from my thoughts.

By the age of twelve, I was already an experienced shot, and was allowed to roam the fields and woods alone with my twenty-bore double-barrelled shotgun and a Remington .22 rifle – something that would cause nightmares to parents and Police in these days sixty years forward.

At my boarding school in Herefordshire, I was not interested in organized games – cricket, soccer and rugger – and, although I was a tennis fanatic, spare time hung heavily on my hands until I discovered the large stream that bordered the school grounds and Colwall Race Course held some large trout which had come upstream from the much larger Cradley Brook. The trout were to be found in the larger pools, and although I tried tickling them I was unsuccessful, and my first commercial interests were aroused.

Now the water in the stream was spring fed, and was so pure that upstream it was utilized by Schweppes for one of their mineral-water bottling plants. Thereafter, some of it was diverted to the outdoor swimming pool of my school, and downstream of all this was the stretch of water that was to be my hunting grounds – a stretch of some 300 yards with 20-foot-high trees and bushes which screened the stream in its small valley from prying eyes. Just the ideal location for illegal operations.

As I could not tickle the fish, nor net them, I decided to build a couple of dams, so that I could stop the flow of water, reduce the level substantially and just lift out the trout floundering in the mud. One must not imagine that the trout were numerous, I was lucky if I caught three in a week, but it was the first challenge of my commercial instinct.

However, first and foremost I had to build the dams. There was plenty of good hard clay available from the banks of the ravine through which the stream ran, but it was rock hard and difficult to quarry. I decided it would have to be blasted. Illegally, I had brought some shotgun cartridges in my playbox and I proposed to use the powder of these for my first experiment with dangerous explosives. Realizing that I needed some kind of flash or detonator to set off the charge, my next move was to take an empty Horlicks Tablet glass file to the school motor mowers, when Harry the groundsman was not looking, and drain off a gill of petrol. Having accomplished this without being seen, I removed the shot from a cartridge and filled that space with cotton wool, to be soaked in petrol. I needed a fuse. Now the school allowed its pupils to buy fireworks for the Guy Fawkes bonfire night, and I had managed to save over some of the slow match that we used for lighting our rockets – normally under school supervision.

So using my Woolworth bit and brace, I bored a hole into the rock-hard clay, inserted the cartridge (plus some more for luck) filled with petrol-soaked cotton wool, attached the slow match to the tamped charge, and lit it just as the Headmaster blew his whistle which signalled all boys were to leave the playing fields and get into class. As we all ran across the playing fields to the school classroom, I heard a distant boom some 300 yards away, and in triumph realized the my first blast had indeed successfully detonated, with what results I had yet to discover. Discover I did, and was very pleased. There had been quite a good fall of first-class dam-building material.

Thus I built the first dam with my chums, all of whom were bound to the greatest secrecy. Into the walls of the dam we built discarded saucepans with the bottoms knocked out, but with the lids remaining. To open the sluices, one just pulled off the saucepan lids which were built vertically into the walls of the dam. Thus it was possible to drain a section of the stream by opening the lower sluices and shutting the upper sluice so that no water entered the section while it drained. Thereafter, the trout were left high and dry or floundering in shallow mud. It was possibly my first excursion into the commercial world.

Genesis

The Headmaster and staff of my school did not take kindly to my enterprise. It drew off interest from school games for, apart from the participation, there are always those in a majority who just want to stand and watch, as in a football stadium of cricket ground. The Headmaster decided to wreck my plans by opening the sluice gates of the outdoor swimming baths which held some millions of gallons, but my intelligence service – the listening ears of the pretty domestic pantry maid – alerted me to the danger. When the school swimming baths were emptied, all my sluices were open, and the flood of water passed harmlessly through the dams. Round One went to me but Round Two was different, which I observed in the School Report to my parents!

Luckily for all concerned, I was due for a public school, being thirteen and so I left the placid countryside of Herefordshire for Wellington College in Berkshire – a military establishment where boys of under fifteen years were kept very much in order.

2

A Military School

There was little place for fishing at Wellington College, where there was greater scope for marching in fours (yes fours!) and doing rifle drill. Certainly there was map reading for military exercises, and I began to study the locality.

I found cricket the most boring game ever, whether watching or playing, and this was the best time of year to get around, but we were not allowed to use a bus or taxi, and the only possibility was a bicycle, but this was no easy acquisition.

If one were a senior member of the Natural History Society of the College, one had the privilege of being allowed to keep one's bicycle for use outside school attendance hours, but how was I, at fourteen, to qualify for this, which was decided on merit or, that is, writing a learned thesis on some form of natural history.

I gave this a good deal of thought, and found that few scholars of my era knew much about Lepidoptera – the study of butterflies. I knew nothing myself, but after pouring over the *Encycolpedia Britannica* and other books in the school library I learnt a lot!

A Military School

Much to the astonishment of my chums, I passed the exam for senior member of the National History Society and had won the honour of having a bicycle. I lost no time in asking my parents to rail my new Raleigh to me! After that, I forgot all about Lepidoptera and have heard little about it since. I had other things in mind.

I was much interested in angling, and although we had five lakes in the school grounds, fishing in them was discouraged for much the same reasons as at my last school. I studied the local papers on sale at WH Smiths in Crowthorne, and there seemed to be possibilities in the Farnham & District Angling Club, of which the Secretary was a barber in Farnham – seventeen miles away, and nothing to me on my cycle, for thankfully there was not the traffic in 1934 that there is now.

I exchanged some letters with the hairdressing maestro, joined the Club, and cycled over to collect my membership tickets, having also applied for one for my chum, John Rawlins. The barber greeted me saying, 'Good Heavens, from the tone of your letters I was expecting a retired Indian Army Colonel, not a schoolboy!' I didn't know whether to be flattered or chastened, but anyway I was now a fully fledged member of the Farnham Angling Club, who had Frensham Pond, parts of Basingstoke Canal, and top of the tree, the River Loddon.

Saturday afternoon in summer saw most of the school playing or watching cricket, but John and I would be far away, having cycled up to 40 miles through the Berkshire countryside, and usually on the Loddon near Aborfield! We had the most marvellous fun coarse fishing, usually with floats, for perch, roach, carp and gudgeon, which I am now ashamed to say we used for live bait. We had plenty of worms, flour paste, and par-boiled potatoes for carp. I established some 'safe houses' – mostly long-suffering friends of my parents, including a Bishop and a former Primus of the Episcopal Church of Scotland – where we had some excellent meals, and who could vouch without a guilty conscience that we were chasing butterflies, as fishing was outwith our curriculum and membership of the Farnham Angling Club would have been very strictly *verboten*.

For a time, I had given up commercial activities concerned with fish, and had become a real angler but, of course, this was costing money, of which John and I had little enough.

My commercial interests were aroused again, so I combined a bit of smuggling with angling. Older boys like to smoke and drink, but could not obtain supplies. Shops in Crowthorne were forbidden to serve the boys of Wellington on pain of losing the valuable custom they had with the school's newspapers, medicines, groceries and so forth. Therefore, Camberley became the free haven for smuggling, and I would load up my pack with cigarettes and Australian Port and various other 'forbidden fruits'. Luckily, drugs were not in vogue at that time, although we all read books about Sherlock Holmes injecting himself with cocaine. I was never caught on one of these criminal forays, but I had one near miss, when my housemaster – a suspicious but inept old fool – stopped me on my bicycle and asked what I was doing. I told him I was just returning from Bagshot Heath after examining the heather. 'Sounds a strange story, with a dartboard on your back,' said he, but luckily that was the end of the interview. Later that afternoon I delivered the dartboard to my eighteen-year-old client for a handsome profit.

We fished the Blackwater which I think meandered through Sandhurst, and was reputedly well stocked with trout by the Royal Military Academy, but I think we never caught anything other than coarse fish lower downstream.

George V had his Silver Jubilee in 1935, and all boys at the school were allowed a weekend off to attend the Jubilee Ceremonies if they had their name on the college board for this. I duly entered my name, and implored Colonel and Mrs Renny Tailyour who lived at Church Crookham, Fleet, to have me for the weekend and take me fishing. This for me was a huge success, and the Colonel took me to a magnificent stretch of the Whitewater at North Warnborough, where there were shoals of fat, brown trout in beautiful water-meadow settings. One was only allowed to fish dry-fly, and the water was gin clear. I was quite hopeless as a beginner at this art. Each time I cast, the fly landed like a bomb on the water, and the fish scattered in all directions. Colonel John was a very skilled fisher, but he could not hook these wily trout either.

While George V was being blessed in Westminster Abbey, Colonel John retired to his car to listen to the radio and the service, also for the reason that a huge thunderstorm his us at the moment. The rain came down in torrents, lashing the placid water into a neo foam bath with a sudden rush of wind so that the surface of the water was much troubled. Now I was quite an expert with a wet fly, fishing downstream with a long line, but this type of fishing was taboo on the Whitewater.

In seconds I whipped off my dry fly, and changed it to a Greenwells Glory, much favoured on Montrose's South Esk, and started casting downstream with a really long line. Within minutes I had a massive take, which was followed by a wonderful fight with a three pound Brownie. I killed it all right and, as the sky cleared, the rain stopped, the sun came out, the service was over, and the Colonel sauntered downstream to find me the proud possessor of the largest trout I ever caught. He was full of praise and, shortly afterwards, we packed up and went home, eating that magnificent fish the same evening. It took me some ten years before I dared tell him the true tale of the poor trout's demise.

Time passed on, and to everybody's surprise, including my own, I did extremely well in my School Certificate (the then equivalent of the 'O' Levels) through which I obtained the London Matriculation and could have gone to university but I was getting restless at Wellington. I wanted to be a farmer, a soldier or a barrister, but my dad said there was no money on the farm, or in the Army and I talked too much already, so no barrister. He proposed that I should go East and join Mathison Jardine as a tea planter in Assam, or become a Quarry Manager trainee in North Wales! I did not like the sound of either, and I was getting more restless and on the verge of open mutiny at Wellington so something had to be done and quickly.

My dad wrote me that there was a vacancy in a local Salmon Fishing Company in Montrose and they would take

A Military School

me on as an apprentice and, if I was any use, I might become a junior manager in five years.

I really did not fancy the job but I thought I must take it to get away from Wellington. Even in 1937, war clouds were gathering, and I thought I would play for time if I got the job in Montrose, join the Territorial Army, and if war broke out, I would be ready for it. The die was cast.

3

High Jinks in Edinburgh

I left my school in Berkshire in December 1937, and I cannot say I was sorry. I had really had enough of it and the school had had enough of me.

The firm to whom I was apprenticed wanted me to get some grounding in ordinary office affairs, and also to learn something about salmon and commercial netting.

Thus, in mid-January 1938, I became a lodger in a nice large house in Colinton Edinburgh, and every weekday morning I attended Nelson College in Charlotte Square where I learnt to touch type, do commercial arithmetic and learn elementary accounting. These sessions ended just before 1 p.m., and, after a snack lunch, I reported to the Salmon Fisheries Inspectorate of the Board of Agriculture for Scotland. The Chief Inspector was the celebrated WJM Menzies, author of many books on salmon, and my immediate boss was PRC Macfarlane, his deputy, who was later to succeed him. The Sub-office of the Inspectorate was in Castle Terrace, and the Head Office at 101 George Street, but even then the cornerstone of St Andrews House had been laid, and thither the Inspectorate went just after my apprenticeship ended.

Nelson College was quite good fun. I think there were around 200 students aged 17–22, of both sexes, and we were integrated, although the boys who were outnumbered by about four to one, had some difficulty keeping their end up. The clatter of over twenty manual typewriters in the typing class defies description, and discipline under the long-suffering Miss Barnet was not too good.

I remember one occasion when by pre-arrangement all twenty students loaded their typewriters with round peppermint balls, and were about the type a piece for speed competition. Miss Barnet cried out, 'Now, boys and girls, get ready – go.' Immediately the air was filled with flying supermints which settled like snow all over the classroom, and the chaos was unbelievable! At last order was restored, the peppermints were gathered up or eaten and the typing speed competition got under way.

The commercial arithmetic and accounting, under the Deputy Head, Mr Nelson, was more orderly and there was a great deal less frivolity.

Strangely enough, there did not seem to be a lot of sex play, but then I was not there after teatime, and of course we were all day students with staid (I think) lodgings or homes to go to in the evenings. Actually, most of the students worked from home.

The education at Nelson College was pretty good, and excellent value. My father paid around £5 per term of three months for my studies, which took me up to the Elementary, Part III stage of the Royal Society of Arts.

My duties at the Fishery Board for Scotland were far from

heavy. Mr Menzies seemed to spend quite a few afternoons fishing the Tweed, while Mr Macfarlane played regular golf at Longniddry, leaving us to hold the fort. This does not mean that Menzies and Macfarlane neglected their job: the Board was pretty efficiently run.

There were three adults in my department, of which I was the junior and learner. Apart from learning salmon, I became an expert high-speed tea maker, both for our own staff and the Ministry of Health on the floor below. We had an adding machine (a very new innovation in 1938) and the Department of Health did not have one. As I became proficient in its use, I often added up the TB statistics of the Borders in exchange for 'Big Eats' from the Department of Health on the floor below!

Suffice it to say that I did learn quite a lot about the natural history of salmon and sea trout, and something of the salmon fishery laws, and was there six months, and parted from my superiors on excellent terms.

My parting from Nelson College was less amicable, for some of us were high spirited, and had the beginnings of vandals! I was not all that popular with Mr Nelson Junior, nor his father, who was the principal of the college.

Having taken my exam for the Royal Society of Arts Part III Elementary, I was due to leave the College in August 1938 and start with Joseph Johnston & Sons Ltd in Montrose.

On the day I left Nelson's I could not help playing a disgraceful practical joke on poor Mr Nelson Senior. Now, Nelson College was a tall four-storey building in Charlotte

Square, and a square staircase led to the top of the building, with a wide open space for the centre around which the staircase climbed. On the ground floor was a huge boardroom-type table in the middle of the open space. Mr Nelson was apt to sit there, in his ornate business suit and bow-tie, and interview clients, presumably students and their parents. The table was so large, that Mr Nelson sat really under the high stairs and was invisible from the bannister above, as were his clients. All one could see from the bannisters on the third floor – there were no lifts – was the huge expanse of table, and the droning of voices. On my last morning I had bought a huge fat turbot full of roe from Johnston Green in South Charlotte Street, well concealed in its brown bag, and carried it up with my books to the third floor. Over the bannisters, I could see the bare table, and hear the voice of Mr Nelson Senior talking to invisible figures at the other end of the table. Taking the turbot out of its bag, I dropped it! Down, down it went, and burst on the table below. Roe and guts flew everywhere, while I legged it to the fire escape. Luckily I was into George Street before anyone realized the cause of the explosion, or the likely perpetrator. Legging it back to Waverley Station, I collected my luggage and caught the train back to Montrose. My student days were over.

I never heard from Nelson College again, and they never sent on my Certificate of passing the RSA exam. I had really blotted my copy book. I am not surprised; they just did not want to know me any more.

The period in Edinburgh had been a very useful experience, for I had known little of town life before, being a real country lad, living a mile from the village and six miles from Montrose, with no transport other than a bicycle.

I had a month to get organized before I reported for work with Johnstons. I was seventeen and a half and had managed to pass my driving test in my father's car. I really needed a vehicle to get to work and back home.

My entire capital at that time was around £50 in Post Office Savings Certificates which I cashed. I found a 1933 Vauxhall 14 in Jackson's Garage in Aberdeen for £35, and this I bought. Sadly I could not afford £50 for the second-hand Chrysler Drop Head Coupé alongside it. Now at last I had wheels for work.

4

An Apprentice Starts

I reported for my first regular job at the beginning of October 1938 at the America Street Offices of Joseph Johnstons & Sons Ltd in Montrose. I started by having an interview with the three directors – ex-Provost W Douglas Johnston OBE, John Stansfeld and Graham Smart – and then I was handed over to John Coull, the Superintendent of Salmon Fishings, who was to instruct me in learning the practical side of commercial salmon fishing from the bottom up! I was to work under him in the mornings, and to study company reports and records in the Chairman's office in the afternoons.

I started off in the net loft learning to weave 'leaders'. David Torrie, predecessor of John Coull, acted as my tutor in this complicated new task. Leaders were straight lengths of netting used as curtains to lead the salmon into the bag nets. Learning to weave nets for these straight curtains was comparatively easy, except learning how to start the net. Once the correct starting width was woven, it was not all that difficult to produce the next line of meshes and so forth. For my first month, I persevered with weaving the leaders, then tiering, which is a similar type of curtain used for the fly nets. Both bag nets and fly nets, into which the leaders or tiering guide the fish, are a series of traps, shaped like a 'V', with the entrance getting smaller into the final pocket of 'Court' into which the salmon is virtually trapped, swimming free. It is fairly rare for the fish to find their way out. The pocket traps, being shaped like Vs, require quadrilateral-shaped tops and bottoms, and therein lies a more complicated application of weaving to produce not a curtain but a quadrilateral-shaped piece of netting. This is produced by a process known as 'taking in and letting out' and it was a month or so before I mastered this.

The mesh size was produced by knitting over a gauge, the minimum for catching salmon was a 3½" mesh, and the nets were measured regularly by the Salmon Superintendent with a 'gauge' or wooden plug. Woe betide the weaver if the knots slipped or a mesh of 3" or 4" was inaccurately produced!

The bag nets in 1938 had steel-wire moorings and, because the steel tended to rust and corrode in salt water, it had to be covered in spun yarn, which was wound round the steel manually with a serving mallet; a very slow and time-consuming job.

The nets used in commercial sea fishing were mostly mounted on manila ropes, and these had to be cut and spliced to the right dimensions. Similarly, the steel-wire ropes had to be cut and spliced, and this was a very painstaking, skilled job done with a steel marlin spike.

In 1938, Johnstons brought their own cotton in beams from Lancashire and spun this into twine in their own cotton

An Apprentice Starts

works, known as a twine shed. The Foreman of the twine shed was an Irish bachelor, David Kelly, who was imported from Ireland with the machinery! He was a crusty man of around 50 when I joined Johnstons, and had anarchist tendencies. He was at war with just about everybody from the Directors to the Apprentices, but for some strange reason he took to me, and was always very helpful in instructing me in his art! It was a very skilled process, and the foreman had to have an excellent knowledge of his machinery. He was assisted by three youths, who, like me, were really apprentices. Johnstons not only spun their own twine into different gauge twine – about five sizes were in use – but then had the nets hand woven by outworkers in their own cottages on piece rates.

Complete salmon nets ready for fishing in the sea were thus produced, not only for Johnstons' own use (at this time they were far the largest operators of fixed sea-salmon nets in the UK), but the firm also sold complete kits to smaller operators, known as 'tacksmen'. Besides learning all about weaving, spinning and net mounting, my morning duties included instruction at the 'carpenter's shop' where *all* the boats for Johnstons' operations were produced from river cobles of 8′ length to motorized sea cobles of 28′, all under the direction of the Carpenter – the Foreman – Duncan Christie and his staff of three.

Duncan Christie became another very close friend of mine, chiefly because we both had a passion for shooting and wildfowling on Montrose Basin. Not only did I learn quite a bit about boat building from him, but also the types of wood he required for his craft and the purchasing skills required to acquire suitable timber: mostly larch, oak, elm and ash for boat building, and imported whitewood for oars, scum handles and other tools of the trade.

I do not want to bore the reader with all the intricate details of the trade I was learning but this outline will give some idea of the complexity of skills required for large, commercial sea-salmon fishing in 1938.

My afternoons, as I have said, were mostly spent studying the history of Joseph Johnstons & Sons Ltd, reading up many law cases regarding poaching and illegal fishing and getting some idea of accounting and bookkeeping. Once or twice a week I would accompany the Chairman, Douglas Johnston, to the farm which the company ran at Kinnaber and I was obviously being groomed to work under him, not only with cropping and animal husbandry but in elementary land management, measurement and general farm maintenance.

From the beginning of October 1938 to the end of January 1939, I had plenty of occupy my time in America Street in the period when it was the salmon close season; no salmon catching was taking place. It was a time for preparation. I lived a typical office life nine to five for five and a half days a week, and took my hour's lunch break in the town. There was not much time to do anything else, but I was enjoying it.

Rather eagerly I looked forward to getting some real marine experience when preparations for the season opened on 1 February 1939.

5

The Rudiments of Sea-Salmon Fishing in 1939

Montrose Bay, which extends from Milton Ness to Scurdiness Light House, was in 1938 the most productive area for its size in the whole of the United Kingdom for that king of fish, the salmon, and this was where the fortunes of Joseph Johnstons & Sons Ltd, were made, and were to remain so for the next forty years.

The North Esk and the South Esk were at that time among the first ten productive salmon rivers in Scotland, and the salmon, grilse and sea trout left for far-off feeding areas to seek the rivers and pools of their birth, where they found a safe resting place (poachers permitting!); that is those that survived the coastal and river nets and the seals.

There are only two types of salmon netting practised in Montrose Bay. In legal terms, they are known as 'fixed engines', but to the more practical they are bag nets and fly nets.

Fly nets are those used in shallow water, and this netting is mounted on wooden stakes, 17′–19′ peeled larch poles,

A Salmon Fisher Remembers

Fishing a fly net.

which are implanted to a depth of up to 4' in the sand. these stakes are rigidified by guy ropes, attached to 5' wooden pins or posts, which are peeled larch of roughly 3" in diameter. These pins are embedded in the sand to a depth of around 3' 6" so that a 1" guy rope can be attached to the exposed 18" of the pin, and secured about 4' from the top of the stake. Horizontal ropes are attached to the stakes which not only preserve the distance between each, but rigidify the structure further and permit the fishermen to walk along the framework to fish the net at the pockets or traps. As previously explained these traps are V shaped making it very difficult for the fish to escape.

Bag nets are in reality little more than floating fly nets, and are used in deeper water where the minimum depth of water exceeds 10'. They can be used in any depth of water, including the multi-fathom sea lochs or open sea of West Scotland. Salmon, being surface swimmers, seldom cruise more than 12' below the surface. These bag nets are kept in position by mooring ropes attached to anchors and steel eye bolts on rocks where the bottom is rock rather than sand. Corks are used to float the nets. Many of the nets have bottom ropes made of 1½" flexible steel-wire rope, and this keeps the nets open for fishing. To prevent the net operating in the weekly close time, the tops and bottoms, which were held open by wooden spars during fishing time, are loosened and the top and bottom laced together so that no fish could enter the nets. This process, which included removing the leaders, is known as 'slapping'. All netting for salmon in the sea had to be removed during the annual close time, and all the stakes of the fly nets, so that when the season was about to open, there was a vast amount of preparation to be done before the nets could operate.

Ashore with the fly net catch.

Thus it was on a cold windswept shore near Montrose in February 1939 I had my first experience of these preparations.

I was detailed to assist the Rossie Station, just off the town of Montrose, and the fly net we had to plant that day was known as The Annat Inshore. This was the inshore pocket of nets or 'head' lying nearest the high-water mark. As the season progressed, four more 'heads' would be added seawards to make the length of the Annat, from inshore to furthest point offshore, a distance of at least 350 yards.

First of all, we had to carry stakes, one at a time, on the shoulders of each man, from the conical pile of stakes at 'The

a fly net. George Thomson, salmon fisher first class, at Rossie station, Montrose, 1958.

The Rudiments of Sea-Salmon Fishing in 1939

Bothy' across the sand dunes, and, from the high-water mark muster, down a distance of fifty yards, dropping off the stakes at intervals as told by our Foreman, David Adams. Once the stakes had been laid out, they had to be up-ended and inserted into the sand with their broadest, sharpened end. This operation known as 'plantin', was done with a tool of massive proportions shaped like a marlin spike. It was 3' high, made of conical-shaped wood, with a shaped steel conical point. Through the shaft, or stake, of the 'gurrl' ran a steel shaft, protruding some 4' either side of the main shaft. The gurrl was used for planting pins as well as stakes, and was operated by up to eight men. The scheme was to insert the point in the sand and then rock this instrument to and fro, while its weight, about 5 cwt, kept slipping down deeper into the sand to make a hole. The gurrl was then quickly withdrawn before the sand slipped in from the side and the pin or stake quickly inserted. This was then rocked to and fro a few times to let it sink into the hole just made, and hopefully to take it down a few further inches. This was all very hard manual work. The stakes weighed over 1 cwt, and carrying them over the sandy dunes, and across the dry shifting sand for up to 300 yards without a rest, with our feet in thigh waders, was a very exhausting task, particularly for an undersized youth of barely eighteen years old.

I have explained how the stakes were 'planted' on the sands, but the planting of the pins was equally skilled. Those pins would normally be sunk down to 2' 6" in the sand, leaving from 2'–3' above the sand. To give these a firmer grip, a ring of six men stood round the pin after it had been inserted after boring with the gurrl. These six men were all armed with 'mells' or quasi-sledgehammers with rounded hitting heads; really like a steel fence mallet with a long handle. As soon as a salmon fisher had inserted the pin into the sand, the ring of six men started to drive it down, hammering in very quick succession. It was a very skilled operation, as any error would bring down the hammer on another, if the six did not keep perfect time as they struck the head of the pin in clockwork rotation. It was indeed an awe-inspiring sight to me as a tenderfoot when I hammered in my first pin as a member of the six-strong team. I remember on my first day a fisher from Ferryden, David Dick, then aged about 35, threw his cap on the pin. In about four second flat the base of the cap had gone and the wrecked garment slid down the pin like a dog collar! Thus I learned the planting of fly nets in the hard way, particularly when the fifth head of the Annat lay 400 yards from the shore, and the stakes had to be carried non stop, one per man, for the high water mark. It was pure manual labour; not even horses and carts.

Preparing the bag nets was no easy matter either, and, being done by boat instead of dry land, was a more intricate operation than planting a fly net. Much of the skill lay in mooring the net in the correct position and getting the anchors to hold, in view of the fearful storms that rage in the open sea off the east Scottish coast. The position of the anchors was buoyed with small wooden barrels which were specially made for the job. These were strapped with manila rope and left with an eye for securing to the mooring wires or anchors. The bag nets were usually set in a predetermined fixed position

...ents of Sea-Salmon Fishing in 1939

Fishing a bag net in Lunan Bay, 1949.

which had been discovered over many years of trial and error, and special wooden marks were often erected on shore to give the lines and transits for the positioning of the nets.

In 1939 Johnstons employed around 200 sea-salmon fishers from roughly Stonehaven to Kirkcaldy, but a large proportion of these men worked in Montrose Bay. In Johnshaven and St Cyrus a majority of the manual workers were salmon fishers, and immediately after the 1939–45 War, Johnstons were easily the largest single employer of labour in Montrose, while Chivers, the jam makers across the street, were the largest employers of female labour!

Fly nets all had special names, The Annat, The Bothy, the Spout, Maryfield, The Soutar, The Cove, Midline, and so forth. One man was responsible for fishing his fly net, twice a day, 5½ days a week, and normally 4 to 6 fly nets were

Salmon transportation: pannier pony on Woodston cliff path.

under a foreman. Each 'station' usually carried one or two spare hands for mending damaged nets or covering during sickness, and these men were responsible for getting the salmon caught to the local collecting point. They were carried in creels, or in specially made sacks, carried by the men on their bicycles. When I joined Johnstons, all the fishing of fly nets was done by manual work, except at Lunan Bay and Woodston Cliffs, St Cyrus, where a donkey or 'Jenny' was employed to carry to salmon up the steep cliff paths.

The bay-fishing cobles were built by Johnstons, and with three exceptions were totally manual; that is, rowed by oars, although one at Elie had a drop keep and a sail. The three

The Rudiments of Sea-Salmon Fishing in 1939

luxurious motorized cobles were at Catterline, Johnshaven and Gourdon. Like the rowing cobles they carried a crew of six, and were petrol/paraffin engines called Kelvins.

I have tried to describe the rudiments of sea-salmon fishing in 1939 and this has been practised with little change for over 100 years at the time of which I write in 1995. The enormous charges brought about by the replacement of the hand-grinding manual labour by mechanization will become apparent in later chapters of this volume.

6

The 1939 Salmon Season Opens

Having spent the first fortnight of February getting the fly and bag nets ready in Montrose Bay, I eagerly awaited the start of the 1939 salmon-netting season for the North and South Esk Fishery Board Districts.

Johnstons owned or leased all the salmon rights in the North Esk from Marykirk Bridge to the sea. These fishing rights covered both banks of that river for a distance of some four miles!

The jewel in the crown was Morphie Dam Dyke Pool, which was a long deep pool below a weir, or dyke, and this had been built to supply Montrose with its water, as well as supplying a distillery and a sawmill.

The real value of Morphie Dyke was that it effectively blocked the upstream ascent of the salmon, which could only ascend the walls of the weir in special flood conditions. Many salmon swam from the sea up to the Dyke, and then either rested in its calmer water, or fell back to the lower pools to wait for conditions to make the ascent more favourable.

The 1939 Salmon Season Opens

This pool usually held about 2,000 spring salmon in mid-February in the 1930s, which were of enormous value to the netsmen. Under normal conditions, no other firm in the UK could match Johnstons for the supply of salmon at this period, but had they netted the whole pool on 16 February the salmon price in Billingsgate Market would have collapsed. Therefore, it was prudent to net around 150 salmon per day, starting at the tail end of the pool, and working a bit further upstream every day until the resident stock was exhausted; hopefully nearly two weeks at 150 fish per day.

The salmon fishers normally assembled about 5.00 a.m. on 16 February, and shortly afterwards the Directors arrived. This was a traditional ritual, and it was not uncommon for thirty people, including the river bailiffs, to be present on the opening day. Usually the Senior Managing Director took overall charge of the operations and the technical side was directed by the Superintendent of Salmon Fishings, John Coull. 1939 was his first year in that office, and the Senior Skipper under him was John Clark, who lived at the Pondage Cottage under a mile downstream with his house beside the river and his eagle eye on the Dyke!

It was pitch dark when I

River netting on the North Esk.

arrived there before 5.30 a.m. and it was bitterly cold. There was ice along the river banks, although the stream ran free in the centre. There were two huts just below the Dyke, where the nets, boxes and oars were stored. The two river salmon cobles were chained to their moorings at the riverside.

The men went about their preparations in comparative silence; it reminded me of a collection in church! People spoke in whispers, and there were rival factions down among the fishers as to how the operations should be conducted. Woe betide any loud-mouthed tenderfoot should he make an impudent remark.

Although the netting season at that time opened officially at midnight, it was deemed unwise to start too early. For the past few days, there had been a night watch of security men (salmon fishers) patrolling the water to see that poachers did not get in first. Poachers are no respecters of legal close times, so it was necessary to have these extra security men additional to the River Board watchers, on duty from 1 February, when the salmon were beginning to congregate.

One must remember that in 1939 there was no deep freezing and no fish farms, and it was illegal to have in your possession, to sell or to buy salmon from 1 November to 1 February, all through the United Kingdom. Nor could hoteliers serve it, other than smoked salmon. So the poachers were fairly quiescent in the winter months, and concentrated on pheasants, partridges and rabbits.

So back to the scene at Morphie Dyke on 16 February 1939. Around 6.00 a.m., the dry nets had been dipped in the freezing water, and willing and very cold hands began to pile the net on the stern sheets of the cobles, specially designed for the purpose. John Coull would instruct the coble crew at which point to leave the bank, and row for the other bank. A salmon fisher held a rope attached to the net, and started pulling it off the stern of the coble as it rowed across the current and the net 'paid off' from the transom of the boat. When in midstream, the coble turned downstream and when opposite the 'hayling' rowed frantically inshore. A rope like a heaving line was thrown from the boat to the dense crowd of fishers (usually more than four times the number required) who hauled the net end ashore. Meantime, the men holding the other heaving line in the net were walking downstream, pulling the net as close to the bank as they could. More bodies joined the upstream lot and everybody took up a position of great self-importance – from Senior Managing Director to the humble apprentice. Each considered that without their guidance, things would go awry! It was very necessary to keep the weighted ground ropes of the net on the river bottom otherwise the fish would escape underneath the net.

The two ends – extremities – of the net were then hauled ashore, and there would be a terrific splashing of captivated salmon in the 'boosum' of the net, which was specially reinforced to take the strain.

Mini pandemonium then broke loose; salmon fishers waded in to the 'boosum' of the net and cracked the splashing salmon on the head with 'patties'. These were 18" batons, much the same size as policemen's truncheons but less well embellished, in peeled larch. It was most important to hit the salmon on the head – if they were struck on the body the flesh would be bruised and ruined. Woe betide the hasty ignorant lad who hit the salmon other than on the head. It was not uncommon for some of the salmon fishers to sustain wounds themselves.

In 1939, my first season at the opening, around 150 salmon had been netted at the tail end of Morphie Dyke in around six 'hauls', but only a fraction of the pool had been netted. These 150 salmon were boxed at the riverside, with on average about 14 to a box, and each box weighing around 130 lbs. This was the quota for that day at Morphie Dyke, and the time was around 7.00 a.m., with dawn now breaking. While these hectic fishing and 'boxing' operations were taking place, two spare salmon fishers had been acting as cooks and stokers in the Bothies, and the netsmen now adjourned to these two huts where enormous specially made 'Bridies' had been heated up until they were too hot to touch, and where there was a large cauldron of steaming coffee. These 'perks' were provided free by the company, and were much enjoyed by the cold fishers, who now got warmed up. To mark this very special day, John Stansfeld, the company Chairman, provided a bottle of Findlaters Rum for all or any of those who liked it. Surprisingly, only a few of the older men went for the rum. I was really teetotal at that time, but I could not resist a taste, and I must say, I really enjoyed it. It remains one of the few tots of rum I have drunk without forgetting it, even to the name of the bottle!

By around 8.30 a.m., it was time for me to go upstream to Craigo Fishing Station Bothy, where another crew would be fishing the river, again below a dyke, and the long pool 200 yards downstream of it, known as Kinnairdy. George Clark was the skipper here, a younger brother of John who was the gaffer at Morphie. 1939 opening must have been a good one, because in no time we had netted another 150 salmon, when a halt was called. If Johnstons put more than 300 salmon in the market that day, prices would tumble, so they were keeping the rest of the river potential in reserve.

The netting here was over by 10 a.m. and I went off home to a late breakfast. I was due in the office by about 11.30 and by 1 p.m. I was free to lunch in Montrose, which would cost me around two shillings in those days. After lunch, I was free until 4 p.m. when a meeting would be held as to how netting was to be done on the following day, and roughly how many salmon would be required. Here I enjoyed a very great privilege in being allowed to fish for salmon anywhere I liked on the North Esk from Morphie Dyke to the sea! The pools were teeming with salmon in these days. Fishing with other than fly was rather frowned upon, and although I rarely fished for more than two hours in the afternoon, I seldom failed to catch a salmon.

After returning to the office for the late afternoon briefing, it was really routine to follow the general pattern of the morning before, and thus the netting of Morphie Dyke proceeded for around ten days, with an expected yield of around 2,000 salmon before numbers were down to lesser figures.

Craigo and the Canterland fishings opposite were not yielding nearly so many salmon, but their river net fishings would continue until 31 August, and the whole river would have had the 'once-over' from April or before, so the crews would not settle on Craigo Dyke and Morphie Dyke only, but fish down the whole river. There seemed very little demand for salmon angling in those days, and the North Esk right up to Loch Lee produced very poor catches of rod-caught salmon and grilse. Notwithstanding, there was magnificent angling to be had from Morphie Dyke to the sea for at least the first six weeks of the season. The Directors caught a few salmon, but at that time seemed to have more important things to do.

Up to 1939 I had only caught one salmon in my life, fishing the Crathes Castle water on the Dee, where I was a chum of Roger Burnett, the son of the Laird, Major General Sir James Burnett of Leys. I was also very impecunious, and the only salmon tackle I possessed was 30-year-old green heart rods belonging to an uncle, who had perished with his ship in 1912 when crushed in the Arctic ice. These rods were very old and clumsy, usually about 17' long! Nevertheless, I did kill a few salmon with them. One afternoon, I was playing a really heavy fish in the Pondage Pool, when up came a very smart chauffeur-driven Daimler with ex-Provost Douglas Johnston and his dog coming to take the air and have a look at the river. He watched me play the fish, and then there was a loud crack and the old rod split, and the top splashed into the water. I can't remember whether I ever landed the fish, but Douglas Johnston had clearly seen what had happened. We did not speak, because I was midstream in my waders, and by the time I reached the bank, he was gone. I thought little more of the incident, and no doubt decided to try out another of my uncle's old rods, that is until . . . !!

The 1939 Salmon Season Opens

A few days after this incident, Douglas Johnston told me I was to report to WJM Menzies, the celebrated Chief Inspector of Salmon Fisheries, at his office just before 1 p.m. in Edinburgh. Mr Menzies took me to lunch, then to Hardys, the famous salmon-fishing people who had a shop in George Street. Menzies selected the most expensive split-cane fly rod they had in stock, a 14' 6" Palakona, then chose a reel and line, and taking the tackle out to a side street, started casting with it. Imagine what would happen if one tried to do this today! Anyway, he seemed pleased with his efforts and with the tackle, had it all parcelled up, and told me that it was a present to me from Douglas Johnston, who had briefed him of my broken rod, and told him to provide me with the best that money could buy! It was an extremely kind gesture, and something I treasure to this day, for I still have the tackle and, although I no longer use it, I would never part with it.

Just before I had acquired this magnificent rod, I did try out something of my own. I had bought a split-cane grilse spinning rod and with it a cheap Bakelite reel, known as the Helical Twin, for around £2.50. (If this sounds like cheap remember that an Illingworth thread line reel – the ace of the light spinning reels at the time – only cost £5.) This Helical Twin used a silk thread line, and I thought I must try it out with a spoon in the Pondage Pool where I had broken the green heart rod.

I tried this out one morning at about 8.30 after I had been present at the netting of Morphie Dyke, and in no time I had hooked a really big fish in the Pondage Pool. I was wearing my waders, and I was nearly in midstream, but I did not want to come ashore until the fish was played out – there were too many tree roots and snags sticking out from the bank.

Although it was 8.30, Mrs Clark, the skipper's wife, had spied me from a window, and came rushing out in her slippers to help. She waded into the river, and I shall never forget my surprise when her skirts filled and billowed on the surface of the pool! She valiantly tried to catch the fish by the tail, but in the excitement that followed, the line broke, and the fish swam away! Sadly we both left the river rather mortified, and Mrs Clark died shortly afterwards. I only hope that this early dip had not been to her detriment.

But enough of the River North Esk, the netting and angling, and off to the sea, where the Johnston Empire held sway from Catterline in Kincardineshire to Kirkcaldy in Fife.

7

Sea-Salmon Fishing, 1939

There was much to learn about the deep-water netting for salmon in 1939: methods had changed little in 150 years. The standard type of net was a bag net, and these had to be fished from a boat, or coble as it was called. Cobles were flat-bottomed crafts with no keel, so that they would not catch the nets when they sailed across them. With four exceptions all Johnstons' sea-going craft were rowed – either by six men, or smaller boats by four men. They varied from 27′ to 18′. The four exceptions were at Elie, Catterline, Johnshaven and Gourdon. The Elie coble had a sail and a drop keel and, as it covered a large area of the Forth estuary, this was a big help. The other three cobles were engined by Kelvin petrol paraffin inboards driving propellers through a tunnel, with a grid or grill built flush with the flat bottom of the coble, this again being necessary so that the craft did not snag the nets. Cobles were built of larch on elm frames, and the gunwales and rubbing strakes were of ash. All the boats for the next 25 years, rowing and motorized, were built in Montrose under Duncan Christie, the foreman carpenter, who originally hailed from Gourdon. He was truly a master of his craft, and although I saw many other cobles built by others in the next 48 years, I never saw one to rival the work of Duncan, be it a 14′ river rowing coble of a 26′ seagoing craft with inboard engines.

During the spring and early summer of my first year, I spent much of my time at sea, learning to splice ropes, lay moorings, shift anchors, put in leaders and remove them, and, most important of all, fish the nets.

I was relatively a greenhorn at sea, although my father's younger brother had been quite a celebrated explorer and sealer in the Arctic, where, as previously stated, he lost his life in the Hudson Strait in 1912. Some of his crew had hailed from Gourdon, and he was well known in Johnshaven and Dundee, and even the mention of his name brought forth a good response and help from the local fishermen. One of his dinghies the *Four Sisters* (they were my aunts) had been preserved as a sort of memorial to him in Johnshaven, and one of his ships, the *Snowdrop*, also previously lost in the Arctic ice without casualties, was portrayed in the Ship Hotel of Johnshaven.

I mention my uncle, Osbert Clare, because I was determined to learn about the sea, and as I was really alone in this, I needed the contacts, and it was through Osbert Clare that I got them.

Going to sea as a tenderfoot seaman in salmon cobles certainly helped to teach me the job, but I had seafaring ambitions beyond this. I managed to buy a 14′ 6″ rowing boat from Jim Crowe, the Mussel Foreman at the back of Rossie Island, Montrose for £4 15s. and this I determined to motorize. With just about my last £1, I bought a shop-soiled Swedish solo marine single-cylinder petrol paraffin inboard with shaft and propeller for £33. With much help from Duncan Christie and Adam Craig, a friend of his and mill mechanic at Gourdon Mill, the engine was fitted, and trials run.

The boat badly needed a coat of paint, a name and registration. She became the *Compleat Angler*, ME 12, and was splendidly painted by Wattie McBay, a regular salmon fisher from Johnshaven, who was also a very dab hand at painting boats, names and sign boards. While painting the name *Compleat Angler* which he did very slowly, methodically with much sucking and blowing on his pipe, curious sightseers, walking along Esk Road at the back of Rossie Island, Montrose, where I fitted out the boat, remonstrated with Wattie on his bad spelling of 'Compleat'. Wattie carried on without apparently taking any notice, until he suddenly exploded! I can't remember his exact words, but in no time the admiring – or critical! – crowd vanished along the road.

Now the boat was ready for sea, and I needed crew and tutor! I picked Craigie McBay, son of the painter, who was the same age as me, and a salmon fisher employed on the estuary salmon nets in Montrose Basin. He bothied at 1 Esk Road, and my moorings were just 50 yards away from his bothy, so he could also keep an eye on the boat.

Craigie had considerably more experience of the sea, fishing and boat handling than I did, but for a start we tried handlining for cod and saithe off Ferryden, and kept within the estuary limits. We dug the lugworm bait from the sand banks in

Montrose Basin and also used mussels which were grown in great profusion on the mud banks within the estuary. Frank Crowe, the son of the mussel Foreman, lived with his family at the back of Rossie Island and helped to keep an eye on my boat when I was at Ecclesgreig or away on business, and Craigie was always off to Johnshaven for weekends with his parents in South Street. By June, we were both more experienced and full of confidence, and our horizon broadened!

Instead of sticking to the sheltered waters of Montrose Harbour and Estuary, we sailed out of the South Esk River, past Scurdyness, and into Montrose Bay, where we shot our baited lines. This had to be done about 5 a.m., before my company work started, and there were very few folk about at that time of day. Both Craigie and I had profited much from Alec Pert, a full-time railway signalman, who was a part-time fisherman of very considerable experience.

One morning in June, Craigie and I left our moorings and proceeded down river and into the Bay, where quite a rough sea was running. I was to shoot the lines while Craigie attended to the engines, particularly the throttle and gear lever, as our speed through the water had to be rigidly controlled to the speed at which I could 'shoot' the baited lines over the stern. Craigie reduced speed and the engine stalled, and we could not get it restarted. All petrol paraffin engines were notoriously bad starters at the critical temperature between petrol and paraffin. We were alone on the sea, and drifting shorewards, blown by a stiff easterly wind and a rising sea. We drifted towards the Annat Bank, a most dangerous area in stormy weather, with seas breaking on the sands, and

Sea-Salmon Fishing, 1939

a fearsome current flowing out of the Montrose Basin which at times could exceed six knots. Many people had been drowned in the area. We had no lifebuoys nor life jackets.

We were in a most perilous situation when down to our rescue came David Pert, a Ferryden fisherman, who must have seen us pass down river and realized our most dangerous predicament.

David Pert threw a rope to us in the nick of time, and towed us into deep water and away from danger. While under tow, Craigie succeeded in restarting the engine and, after recovering our line, we sailed back unscathed to Rossie Island.

Because of the very dangerous current when Montrose Basin empties, the port is not really suitable for small boats, and I decided to keep my boat at Gourdon, which was much safer and beside the open sea, with an excellent inner harbour for small boats. I bought a shed on the quayside, and our skipper's son at Gourdon kindly agreed to look after the boat for me when I was at home in St Cyrus six miles away.

Without Craigie, I had to manage the boat on my own, and became quite proficient at this. Those fishermen who worked lobster pots and herring nets were mostly retired full-time fishermen, and some of them went to sea in rowing boats. I was eighteen at this time, and became very friendly with a Mr Ritchie, who had herring nets and creels and a rowing boat, which had been the inshore rescue boat at Montrose. It was a heavy unwieldy craft, but Mr Ritchie, who must have been in his seventies, was a hardy soul, who had little difficulty in rowing it. I often towed him in and out, while I learnt daily of his skills. Alex Gove, who was a fish merchant on the quayside, was also very good at giving me advice and helping to look after my gear. James and John Stewart were skippers in the employ of Johnstons much further south but were Gourdon men and I owed quite a lot to John in particular for good advice.

John was lost overboard from a Gourdon fishing boat off the village in the war, and James became the first Secretary Manager of the Gourdon Fishermen's Association.

My stock was high in Gourdon in those days and I had many friends in the village. This was to change dramatically in twenty years' time when I became the most hated man in the village. But more of this anon!

From the foregoing, one might have wondered if I was paying sufficient attention to my full-time job with Joseph Johnstons, but I was young in those days and a working day of ten hours, six days a week was not too strenuous.

While learning the 'nitty gritty' of practical commercial salmon fishing, and bookkeeping, I was also privy to some of the inner secrets of the three Directors, and the Superintendent of Salmon Fishings.

Johnstons leased a coastal salmon fishing from John Stansfeld, the Chairman, and it was common knowledge that Willie 'Codling' Mearns of Ferryden was reputedly fishing Johnstons' nets. Johnstons' Directors seemed hesitant of taking any action.

Now the 'Codling' was a remarkable man, but of limited financial means. In Montrose, Lady Cockerill, the very rich wife of Sir George, was dying of cancer at her palatial residence, Grey Harlings, on the Golf Course, and among the

Sea-Salmon Fishing, 1939

retainers was Nurse Wilkins, who looked after her in her terminal illness.

Somehow Codling got to know her, and persuaded her to have a boat built in Montrose by Arbuthnott & Sons, Boat Builders of considerable repute. This boat would be owned by Nurse Wilkins and fished by 'Codling' and he and Nurse Wilkins would split the profits. Now this was the boat that was reputedly interfering with Johnstons' salmon.

Willie The Codling was falling out with Nurse Wilkins at this time, because she was not getting any profit from Willie's fishing operations, not even the mythical (?!!) salmon from Johnstons' nets. So Nurse Wilkins decided to sell the boat in spite of the hostility of Willie, and she employed Tom Whitson, a well-known Montrose solicitor, to get on with the job. As Willie had sworn to sink the boat rather than part with it, no local could be persuaded to buy it. Already I was well versed in the gossip of Montrose Harbour area, and I suggested to my superiors that they should buy the boat and eliminate the threat to their interests.

Surprisingly, the Directors turned down my suggestion. I do not think they wanted to get involved.

I decided to buy the boat, which went very cheaply because of the circumstances. It was sold for £50, and had cost over £250 new and was under a year old.

Knowing Willie, I knew I had to take the boat by storm. I managed to enrol the Nicholson tribe for transport from Gourdon/Bervie, since they made their livelihood driving blocks of ice from Aberdeen to Johnstons, and delivering beer from Alloa to north-east Scotland. They had a big lorry

– big enough to transport this 24′ boat – and I hired other fishermen allies from Gourdon to make up the 'Shock Army'!

Plans of my purchase were known to Willie, and stealth had to be used. When Willie came in from sea one day, he spied me and Charlie Ross, Fishing Boat Registrar for Montrose Customs, on the quay, and he immediately turned about for the open sea. But he was not cunning enough – he had to return sometime and we were waiting, hidden behind coils of rope and any bits and pieces on the harbour wall. I had already warned Inspector Shewan of Montrose Police that a violent confrontation might take place, and he and Charlie Johnston, a well-known police constable, kept watch from a discreet distance.

Willie Codling and his mate came alongside all unsuspecting, and a boarding party rushed the boat. Insults and curses flew, but no physical violence. Willie was persuaded to come to the Custom House, and a powwow ensued. The 'heavy mob' waited outside the Customs House.

Charlie Ross told Willie that he was now deposed and Michael Forsyth Grant was now the legal owner of the boat. Up till now Inspector Shewan, Constable Johnson and I were silent witnesses of the drama.

When Willie realized he had lost, he picked up a heavy inkwell from the Long Room desk, and flung it at me, at the same time shouting, 'You bastard!' The Inspector and Constable moved in the restrain him, but the Codling fought like a lion. In the ensuing battle, the Custom's desk was shattered, Charlie Johnston's mouth was pouring blood, and Inspector Shewan was winded. Willie rushed past them and left by the door, where he tried to fight my heavy mob. He was felled by a blow to the head, and while he was dazed, he was arrested by the Police. Even then, he was not finished.

As the lorry with the boat on board was driven past on its way to Ecclesgreig, Willie's associates tried to lie down in the street to stop the lorry. It was all in vain, and Willie was locked up overnight in the Montrose nick! Next day he appeared on a breach of the peace charge – strangely enough not a police assault charge, probably because there was violence on both sides.

Willie was unrepentant when he was found guilty. I think he was only reprimanded, but his last words were 'I am leaving this wicked town', a quotation which was printed in the Montrose papers.

He did not leave the town, but survived many more years to fight me again, but this is a later story.

The boat left Montrose, never to return there.

8

An Apprentice in the Making

Apart from learning the day-to-day business of commercial salmon fishing, the Directors were anxious that I should learn something of the future.

In May 1939, I was instructed to assist in the marking of 10,000 salmon smolts, about to migrate from the River North Esk to the sea and these smolt were wont to live in the brackish water of the large Nab Pool before taking the final step into the North Sea far beyond.

This operation was under the direct supervision of PRC Macfarlane, Deputy Chief of the Salmon Fishing Inspectorate in Edinburgh, and my part boss when I was a student there. About five of us were involved – Macfarlane, John Coull (the salmon Superintendent), Roland Milne (the senior skipper on the river), a spare hand and myself. We netted the pool with a very small mesh net, and in it we caught salmon, grilse, sea trout and finnock – and many smolts! Everything except the smolts was released unharmed and there followed the very slow process of marking each smolt. First we cut off the adipose or rear fin, then stuck an aluminium wire under the dorsal fin and twisted it in the manner of sealing a cherry brandy bottle. It made quite a neat job and did not appear to worry the smolt. Working almost full time several days a week, the operation lasted over a fortnight and hopefully most of the smolts made safe passage to sea.

It was a very painstaking and back-breaking business marking these smolts, as we were standing in the river with the flowing water up to our knees all the time and never anything to sit on! Certainly we took the odd meal break, and during one of these I used my .22 rifle to shoot one of the terns, which plagued the area, diving onto the shoals of fish and often rocketing skywards after the dive with a smolt in its mouth.

I examined the shot tern in front of our team, and we were aghast to find three marked smolts in its innards! It goes to show how many smolts were killed in this way, and it may have been that our operation weakened the small fish for a period which made them easier victims. Once we had completed the operation, Mr Macfarlane said he expected and hoped for a return of 200 adult salmon or grilse out of the 10,000 that we had marked, the earliest due to return in about two years' time.

Another ploy I was sent on was to accompany the retired Superintendent of Salmon Fishings, David Torrie, on a 'look see' at the operations of our competitors on the North Kincardineshire Coast between Stonehaven and Aberdeen. There were about seven salmon stations on this coast: Newtonhill, Portlethen, Muckle Shore, Altens, Cowie, Cove and Nigg. These were all deep-water stations, fished by large motor cobles out of the harbours or coves, and it was the first time

I had ever seen a Blondin. This was a remarkable crane-type piece of equipment with a pulley and hook travelling on a rigid wire spanning the coves. Using certain controls, with power supplied by a stationary petrol engine in the Blondin House, loads of up to 7 cwts could be placed in the cobles hundreds of feet below the rigid wire, and consisted of nets, spars, boxes, anchors and so forth. Then salmon, nets and empty fuel drums could be uplifted from the coble moored below and brought up to the Blondin House for onward despatch by road. The Blondin was an ingenious piece of equipment, and I have never seen it used for any purpose other than this, but it may well have had other uses. David Torrie was an excellent instructor, and I profited a lot from what I saw and what David told me. This experience would come in useful fourteen years later. Little did I know this at the time, and we shall return to this later.

We had almost been at war with Germany in September 1938, and this threat was not far away throughout 1939, and, of course, became reality in September that year.

I had always fancied the Army and even the tales of my father, who was a Seaforth Highlander in the trenches in 1914–16, until he was so badly shot up and gassed that he was medically downgraded to command Prisoner of War Camps, had not damped my enthusiasm. My father had been pretty lukewarm over my ambitions, maybe drawing on his own appalling experiences in the Western Front trenches, but I suspect also he considered the Army was very badly paid!

Anyway, I still had ambitions, and early in 1939 asked the Directors if I could join the Territorials. This they flatly

An Apprentice in the Making

refused, but were very keen that I should join the Naval Reserve in Dundee, because not only would I learn about the sea, but also could do my training in the part of the year when there was no salmon fishing, as opposed to the Territorial Army where I would have had military training and camps in the peak salmon catching time. So in April 1939 I became a midshipman in HMS *Unicorn* in Dundee with the Directors' blessing!

At the height of the grilse fishing John Stansfeld took me under his wing to visit our salmon stations in Fife. We had St Monans, Elie, Kincraig, Largo, Lundin Links and Kinghorn. John was extremely good in showing me all the problems, and we stayed at the Marine Hotel in Elie which was a great luxury to me. All expenses were paid by the Company, as my wage was £1 per week and would not have gone very far in the august hostelry!

The two highlights of my first visit to Fife I shall never forget. The first was when we paid a visit to our Kincraig Station; Skipper Stephen had just been stung by a red jellyfish in his eye. It was a most painful injury, but fortunately within 24 hours he had recovered, with frequent eye baths, but it taught me to beware of any personal contact with red jellyfish.

At certain times of the year, jellyfish got caught up in hundreds in the salmon gear, and not only could their presence and weight destroy the efficiency of bag nets and leaders, but would also scare off salmon and sting those in the nets, reducing the value of the fish for market.

The second incident occurred in fog while John and I were embarked in the Elie sailing coble, and were well out into the Forth estuary. Coming out of a fog bank, we were nearly run down by the most modern battle cruisers of the period, the *French Dunkerque* and *Strasbourg*, which were on a courtesy visit to Rosyth.

Our highest station upstream on the Forth was Kinghorn, where we had two fly nets operated by the brothers Blues from Johnshaven. They were a splendid pair of men, aged well over 60, and they ran this station together from the bothy, which was adjacent to a bottle factory! The old boys were very much *persona grata* with the factory, and we were shown over the factory by the Blues brothers who, from their attitude, might have been joint Managing Directors of the factory! We were made most welcome.

Even three weeks before the outbreak, there must have been strong rumours of impending war. I remember going with John Stansfeld to a road haulage contractor and making tentative plans for the collection of our Fife salmon if there was a shortage of transport or petrol rationing.

9

Salmon Fishers in Wartime

The close of the salmon fishing season in 1939 at the end of August was pretty chaotic. War with Germany was almost certain, and those of us who were regular reservists – mostly RNR – had already left for the Armed Services. This was virtually the end of the salmon fishing for us for the duration, and it included John Stansfeld and myself, leaving Douglas Johnston and Graham Smart to run the company.

After a spell in a battleship in Scapa, I was posted to a minesweeper on Loch Ewe, and here I met Chief Petty Officer 'Coullie' Paton, who was a Gourdon Trawl Skipper, and Petty Officer George Henderson of Ferryden whose father had been a cooper for Johnstons. We were all great friends, and were often at sea together when 'Coullie' and George brought trainees to the minesweeper for training classes.

By May 1940 I was cruising in the Minches when I received a letter from John Stansfeld who was serving as a captain in the Gordon Highlanders in the front line in France. I was horrified to read the contents of his letter, which implied that the Germans were advancing at breakneck speed through

France and he could easily fall into enemy hands – and we in West Scotland thought we were winning the war!

Sadly, John's prediction was right, and he was captured with many of his men at St Valery, to have a long and pretty horrific five years in captivity as a POW. He would be sadly missed.

As for myself, I was soon transferred to a new destroyer building in Glasgow. First we went to work up for battle experience in Scapa Flow. Jim Stewart, who had been Johnstons' skipper at Commieston, was now a Chief Petty Officer in HMS *Mount Ard* at Scapa, and I was able to visit him in the destroyer's motor boat for a great 'get together'. The destroyer, *Tynedale* was then sent into the thick of it, being in the first destroyer flotilla at Portsmouth, where for the next six months we were bombed almost daily and nightly, and our base ports, Portsmouth and Plymouth, were virtually gutted by the Luftwaffe. There was little time to think of salmon! However, during one five-day leave, I succeeded in getting a smoked salmon from Johnstons which was more then appreciated in our wardroom.

By October 1940, Johnstons were good enough to continue my pay and this was going up by increments annually, and was now £2 per week. I was more than grateful for this which was five shillings a day.

In 1941, I left the destroyer *Tynedale* for a command in Coastal Forces. I was now an Acting Sub-Lieutenant, at 7s. 8d. per day, with additional payment of 2s. for being in command, and 1s. 6d. per day for 'hard lying' money, as we were considered in less comfortable quarters than larger ships.

Salmon Fishers in Wartime

So for the first time my naval pay exceeded 10s. per day. I well remember getting my first monthly cheque in this situation from the Navy. I had never been so well off before!

I spent the next two and a half years in motor gunboats/motor torpedo boats, mostly at Dover, where we saw more than our share of enemy action.

I still kept in touch with locals and salmon fishers. Alastair Soutar, who had been in the 1939 crew at Craigo was my age, and he used to accompany me on angling trips on the Craigo/Canterland stretch of the North Esk when we were off duty and I was trying out the angling. On one occasion, we counted 176 salmon rising between 8.30 and 10.30 p.m., over which I fished without getting a single offer! Now Alastair was an AB in a minesweeper in Portsmouth where I made contact with him.

Three months later I was sitting reading a book in HMS *Hornet* at Gosport when the Hall Porter knocked on my door to say that a Chief Petty Officer would like to see me. In walked Chief Petty Officer Alastair Soutar aged 21! He was soon serving in a large trawler, *The Milford Duchess* of Dover, as Coxwain, and I gave him a thrill one night as I overtook the trawler in my motor gunboat flat out at 44 knots and 20 yards apart from his ship!

During my time in Coastal Forces I was sometimes on leave, and quite rightly Johnstons expected something in return for what they were paying. On one occasion Douglas Johnston asked me to turn out to help the undermanned crew net a pool known as 'The Laddies Hole' under the lower North Water bridge. Believe it or not, one of the first salmon I took out of the net was one of those 10,000 smolt we had marked in 1939. It was rather a thousand to one chance that I should have seen it! The salmon was released unharmed into the main river, for the 'Laddies Hole' was then a dead end of the Kinnaber Lade, through which salmon could not get upstream since the water was screened at Montrose Water Works!

I was also expected to keep up to date on the office work, but it was not easy to get into Montrose, six miles from my home, with no petrol! So I used to ride my horse from home to the St Cyrus sands, ford the river North Esk and gallop along Montrose sands and up to America Street, where I 'garaged' my steed with the local coal merchant, Muir Son & Patton. Bill Kidd, their foreman, watered and fed my horse while I studied Johnstons' affairs under the direction of Douglas Johnston and Graham Smart. Then I rode back at 5 p.m., visiting the shore stations as I went.

I also had time for a bit of angling and caught several salmon in the Morphie stretch of the North Sea.

On one occasion, when I was serving in motor gunboats at Dartmouth, Lieut.-Com. Mark Thornton, a very distinguished destroyer captain and friend of our family, rang me up to say he was going on leave to my parents', could I possibly arrange some fishing? It was about April, when most of the salmon would have been netted out, but there were always a few finnock to be caught. I told Mark I would arrange it with Johnstons, and he had a glorious week, fishing dry fly upstream which was unheard of on the North Esk at that time, and had 72 finnock for his week. I am sure my parents were delighted with a change from the usual wartime diet!

Duncan Christie, the Foreman carpenter, was a regular shooting companion of mine when on leave, and he told me that a year or so after Willie Mearns had been arrested in 1939, he had returned to Montrose and on one occasion had invaded the Johnstons' premises and, after insulting my name in particular, had met up with Provost Johnston and had a go at him. The police had been called and Willie admonished and told never to go inside 3 America Street again.

In the winter of 1942, Duncan and I were goose flighting one evening on Montrose Basin. It was pitch dark, when out of the gloom a well-hooded figure appeared and addressed Duncan, who, when he spoke, was recognized as Willie Mearns, also a wildfowler. Willie rambled on about the iniquities of Johnstons in general and me in particular, ending with 'I'd like to meet that Michael Grant out here!' I kept mum beside Duncan, but of course I was fully armed and could probably have outgunned Willie, but on this occasion I thought discretion was the better part of valour. Willie sauntered off along the mudbank into the gloom but still we were due for a confrontation years later.

Sadly my career in Coastal Forces ended in February 1944 when I was court-martialled in Dover Castle for hazarding and stranding my ship. I made myself extremely unpopular with everybody from the Vice Admiral downwards, for instead of pleading guilty with any further ado, I engaged the Coroner of Ramsgate as my solicitor and a King's Counsel to defend me. The Judge Advocate of the Fleet had to attend, as did three Cruiser Captains and two lesser figures. The court martial started on 16 February 1944, and in spite of the solemnities of the occasion I managed to telegraph Johnstons first thing to wish them a prosperous start to the Montrose salmon fishing season.

The verdict of the court martial was really a foregone conclusion. I was dismissed from my ship and severely reprimanded, which was a very stiff sentence. Since then, captains of nuclear submarines and super destroyers have been found guilty of the same offence, and just been 'reprimanded'! The court made an example of me, and although I was almost suicidal at the time, I came to think later it was one the best things that ever happened to me, as will become clear later in the book! After the court I was sent to serve in a destroyer on the Russian convoy runs – Britain's answer to Hitler and Stalin's 'Penal Battalions'! So to North Russia I went. I got on marvellously with my destroyer captain, whom I greatly admired, and who finally became a distinguished Admiral. I fished in the Kola River for salmon, and shot duck on the outskirts of Murmansk! I also nearly froze to death! Then I went to the blazing heat of West Africa in January 1945 where I successively ran a naval prison, then all motor and sea transport for the West African Naval Command, and finally became Group Commander of the West African Training Squadron, which included HMS *Arran*, of which I was also the Commanding Officer. I had recovered a lot of lost ground since the year before I had been court martialled.

In far-off Sierra Leone, we were astonished when the war ended so suddenly in August 1945, which we, starved of news, expected to continue until 1947. So in February, 1946, two years after my court martial in Dover, I sailed for home in command of HM Ships *Arran*, *Copinsay* and *Oxna*.

It is a long story, too long to be told here, but I arrived quite 'legally' at home on leave in May 1946, and the Admiralty appeared to have lost track of me. I had about six weeks' leave doing nothing, but greatly enjoying myself *until* Douglas Johnston rang me up one day and said he would like to see me next day, and after this told me I must decide whether to continue in the Navy, or return immediately to Johnstons where the Directors were overstrained.

I opted for Johnstons, and took the night train to London and the Admiralty. They had indeed 'lost' me, and were delighted to discharge me that very day and replace me on the Reserve List of Officers! Within days, I had rejoined Johnstons, but the blow in terms of cash and prestige were high. I dropped from £1000 a year to £250, and from bossing 300 men to myself being bossed as a Trainee Manager; so then I became used to the term 'change of circumstances'. I was no longer a rising star in the Navy. I was back as a trainee salmon fisher – Manager or an 'up one' apprentice – and now I took orders, no longer issued them!!

10

Ascending the Salmon Fisher's Ladder

I rejoined the staff of Johnstons before the close of the 1946 salmon season, and John Stansfeld who had suffered some appalling privations in Prisoner of War camps was back too. Provost Johnston and Graham Smart, his nephew, had coped extremely well under very difficult conditions in the war. Most of the able-bodied men of the 18–38 age group were in the forces. There were severe restrictions on access to the shore during the threat of invasion, and the crew of the estuary trout shot had been bombed, machine gunned and wounded. They had been luckier than the wives of Allan and Willie Arbuthnott, the boat builders who lived beside the Montrose railway viaduct, who had been killed in the same attack.

Mills bombs were readily available, to and through the military in those days, and the rivers were regularly bombed by the poachers, who had a very easy market for their poached salmon. Not only were the salmon killed, but the parr and fry also. Pollution was rife on the South Esk, particularly at

Brechin, where war industries were discharging terrible doses of toxic substances into the river. Also, the river-watching staff had been greatly depleted by the loss of manpower. 1945 had apparently been a disastrous trading season for Johnstons, and 1946 had been no better. There seemed to be quite a chance that Johnstons would 'go under'!

It was under these circumstances that I rejoined the company, and things did not look good, and as a result tempers were often frayed. During late January 1947, I had a terrible row with Graham Smart, who was overseeing my book work. It was the last week of the pheasant shooting season, and I had been invited to shoot at Craigo, but Graham demurred when I asked for the day off, as my accounts were in arrears. I went to John Stansfeld and told him I thought I wanted to resign, and get a job in the Merchant Navy tankers, which at that time I could have easily got with my naval experience. As it turned out, John Stansfeld persuaded me to think again, as he predicted better times ahead. He was quite right. So was Graham Smart. I realized later that I had been quite out of order.

The 1947 salmon season opened with renewed vigour. Nearly all the young employees were out of the services, and everything was attacked with a buoyant hope and enthusiasm. Poaching with explosives was still rife, but the white-fishing community never touched 'red fish' at sea; it was quite taboo. So we got through the season and financial year with much better results, to everybody's satisfaction.

My responsibilities were widened, and I became the Chief Timber Buyer for all our boat building, and under-manager of the farming operations of the company, which were really quite a sideline. 1948 came and went, and that great pillar and strength of the company for so many years – Douglas Johnston – died at a ripe old age in his seventies. He left me £1,000 in his will, which was a fortune in those days, and shortly after I was promoted to a junior Managing Director.

I was lucky. 1949 turned out to be an excellent salmon year, and trading results were better than anyone expected. Johnstons was then among the largest salmon producers in Britain, and because deep freezing of salmon was unheard of in those days, the orderly marketing of salmon was paramount to avoiding gluts or famine, insofar as the human element made this possible. We could hopefully keep large stocks in the river, although a flood could undo this insurance, but the sea was far less easily controlled. Nets could be wrecked, or stormy seas could prevent boats going to sea. As marketing was such a major part of the company's business, I had never been entrusted with day-to-day sales, until one day in 1949 when the two senior directors had business out of the district, and I was to be marketing manager for the first time.

It was in a way unfortunate that my first stint in the job coincided with the record daily catch for years – possibly since before the war!

I managed to sell the lot – just! Every fish merchant from St Andrews to Bristol and London must have been brimming with salmon, but what would happen the next day? I would be lucky if I got a single order. What on earth would I do with another big daily catch? Salmon only keeps on ice for a limited time. The elements saved me, and a massive storm developed overnight, preventing boats from going to sea for at least two days, and wrecking many of the shore fixed nets. I had nothing to worry about until the two senior Directors were back and able to take charge again.

By the end of 1949, Johnstons were really back in the money again, and ready to spend it. New houses were built for foremen at Lunan and Kinnaber, and a huge shed built to replace the run-down boat construction area. Johnstons pioneered salmon cold storage and blast freezing, so that in future any temporary glut of salmon could be cold stored and deep frozen until demand picked up. For the first time new regulations were brought in by which it was legal to sell quick frozen, cold-store salmon in the old close season in the United Kingdom which covered some four months of the winter.

Just before we began to mechanize the collection of salmon from the nets dotted along miles of sandy bays, we relied on donkeys or ponies with pannier, to collect some of the fish, notably at Woodston, St Cyrus, Rockhall and Lunan Bay.

David (Dight) Mackie, the Foreman at Lunan, had a rather self-willed donkey stallion. He was the only person who could control it, and because it could be aggressive he struck up a notice 'Donkey Dangerous. Do not feed' beside the paddock.

Now a lady dentist of considerable standing was staying at the Lunan Bay Hotel nearby, and decided to enter the paddock and talk to the donkey. It is known that at certain periods donkey stallions are over-amorous, and female humans should keep clear. What exactly happened to this lady I never discovered. Suffice to say she was quite badly hurt by the donkey and I think hospitalized. She claimed substantial damages.

My colleagues and I summoned the local Eagle Star representative for a discussion and he said he would handle the case through the insurance, and on no account were we, the Directors, to get involved. The lady received no compensation. She was told it was her fault, that the notice was quite clear. We felt very sorry for the lady who had suffered a lot but we were expressly forbidden to make any financial restitution, much as we wanted to, lest it should be shown as accepting some responsibility.

For over a hundred years, there had been little change at sea, with all fly nets 'planted' without any mechanical aids: boats were launched by hand on junker wheels, and recovered at low water on the wheels by winches powered by hand. Nearly all the boats were rowed. All this was the order of the day of which I was placed in charge.

Seagull outboard motors replaced oars. Winches were motorized. The horse and cart which collected the salmon in Montrose Bay was replaced by a Ferguson tractor, and the same tractor, now fitted with a post hole digger, was converted to implant the pins and stakes in the sands. I started with an ex-Army Bren gun carrier for collecting the salmon, but soon changed to ex-Army weasels.

I had managed to buy one weasel from the London motor people, Pride and Clark, for £100, and Charlie Alexander, the haulage king of Aberdeen, trucked it north for £50, which I thought was an extortionate fee and told him so. Three weeks later I attended a Ministry of Supply auction in

Ascending the Salmon Fisher's Ladder

Planting a fly net. George Easton and a Ferguson post hole digger.

Bromley, Kent, and bought three much better condition weasels for £30 each. They even had army petrol in their tanks, and borrowing trade plates I loaded them on to a railway flat wagon at Bromley. The haulage charge by British Railways was £30 for the three, which I duly informed Charles Alexander! These weasels served us well for salmon collection, after being converted from petrol to petrol/paraffin, and Neil Webster, a resourceful young Montrosian of 19 years whom I recruited as fish carter, used to 'swim' the North Esk and collect salmon on both sides of the river.

Salmon prosperity in the fifties benefited from the Mac-Connachie Report, (MacConnachie was an eminent Sheriff

Principal, assisted by various salmon luminaries which included John Stansfeld). There was a tremendous surge in salmon numbers arising from the Report, which was applied in the 1951 Salmon Fisheries Act, with a counter attack on poaching.

Johnstons had the biggest share of salmon fishings in the South Esk and North Esk districts – among the most valuable in Scotland – and the River Bervie, and the three rivers boards were chaired by the three Johnstons Directors, who had the monopoly of their regulation, subject to the Salmon Fisheries Acts. All the District Fishery Board staff were really answerable to Johnstons, and Johnstons alone, so were personally involved in the suppression of poaching.

On one occasion, it was reported that Willie Mearns was at it again. Using a rowing boat and a gill net, he rowed out at night and stretched his net to block the ascent of salmon, and sea trout, across the South Esk where it enters the sea between Scurdyness and Ferryden. The Board staff, headed by Graham Smart and myself, endeavoured to catch him in one of our new motorized river salmon cobles, but Willie was no fool, and was well supported by his cronies in Ferryden. His scouts were positioned on the main road across Rossie Island (the A92) and whenever we crossed the River Bridge, his scouts, knowing the numbers and make of our cars, flashed headlights downstream to let Willie know we were on our way.

In the end, we proved too crafty. We had a secret rendezvous in Montrose railway goods yard, and trespassed on to the railway line and crossed the river by the railway viaduct. Unfortunately, when half way across, along came a goods train, and we all hid in the lattice work of the bridge. The guard's van stopped right opposite me, and I was terrified the guard would see me and the others concealed in the steel lattice. The goods train moved on, and we continued our journey along the main line and then cut across fields to the bottom of Ferryden. The last 300 yards we crawled through a potato field; 'we' being Graham Smart, Superintendent Brown of the Fishery Board and myself. We reached a vantage point where we overlooked the river, and in the dim light, mainly reflected from the lights of Ferryden and Montrose, could see a rowing boat in midstream.

It had been arranged that we would rush the last hundred yards across the beach pebbles and hold the poacher until the police, who had been forewarned to wait unseen in Ferryden, were alerted by Graham Smart who was to blow his whistle

The railway bridge at Montrose.

and launch me as the fittest, and vanguard of the attack, after the poacher. The whistle blew, and I ran like hell for the boat. The oarsman, alerted by the commotion, rowed frantically for the shore, and I arrived at the stern of the boat as it grounded, and leapt into it. The oarsman tried to escape, but my leaping impetus knocked him over on the floorboards and I held him by the throat and lay on top of him until the police and Graham Smart and Bob Brown all arrived together, when Willie was formally arrested. The language was unprintable.

Willie was duly tried and convicted in Forfar Sheriff Court. During his evidence he told the Sheriff that 'the bastard Grant', pointing at me, had tried to murder him, but the Sheriff, transferring his gaze to me for a moment, noting the immaculate pin-stripe suit, starched white collar and black tie, merely remarked 'he doesn't look that sort of person to me!' and Willie was duly sentenced.

We were also plagued by a gang of Brechin/Dundee poachers on the North Esk, who proved almost impossible to catch. The local farmer, John Salmon of Logie, ribbed me one day in Montrose Market of our incompetence in nailing them. I told him if he supplied the details by telephone the next time he saw the gang, I would reward him with a salmon. 'OK,' he said, 'a salmon for a Salmon.'

I then approached Superintendent Wright of the North Esk Fishery Board, and told him of our deal. He was most eager to nail the miscreants, and was fully receptive when I rang him a few nights later to say that Jock had seen the poachers in the gloom approaching Morphie Dyke.

I was not present when the incident took place, but Isaac

and the police intercepted the men on the job, and arrested all but one, who escaped across a turnip field. A remarkably fit constable pursued him at the gallop and rugby tackled him in the turnips. The whole gang appeared in court and were duly convicted.

I told my two colleagues of my deal with Jock when we were discussing the arrests, and said we would now have to give a salmon to Jock Salmon. They were horrified in that I was bribing someone for information. I told them if the Company wouldn't give the informant the salmon, I would have to pay for it myself. They gave in, and Jock received the salmon with the Company's compliments.

Thus I started a precedent in buying information. It paid off time and again, and at the height of the Drift Net War I was paying out not salmon but thousands of pounds! John and Graham thought it was all most ungentlemanly, and when Mr Braid, the most searching and honest partner of Mackay Irons, CA, of Dundee asked what these payments to Mr Grant were, they replied, 'Ask him. We don't want to know.' Nor did they and the reader will get some idea of the scale of these operations later, for this is the first time that this has been published.

I had acquired a good knowledge of explosives from my war days, and had become quite an experienced – and licensed – dynamiter.

A wartime gun emplacement on Lunan Sands had become a nuisance to us, and it was believed poachers and thieves used it to spy on our operations, and steal fish from the nets, and it was decided to blow it up.

I demurred. It was a big job, and I suggested the local Territorial Army would do it. They tried, but did not succeed and it was left in a most dangerous condition, likely to fall in and kill someone inside.

Most reluctantly, and in a lot of trepidation, I undertook to do the job, with the help of Angus Smart, the then Foreman. I used very heavy charges, as I did not want to crawl under the debris a second time, and the structure was demolished to everyone's satisfaction.

I was then asked to do the same to a large underground bunker at the bottom of Ferryden, built in the war by the Polish Army. It was used by the locals for sex and drug parties, which was in no way connected with salmon fishing!

I refused to have anything to do with it. Wisely I think. As far as I know it is in use to the present day.

11

The Golden Age of Scottish Salmon

In the half century or more that I was involved in salmon fishing – both angling and commercial netting – I think 1952–77 was the Golden Age. Not only were the catches enormous by present standards, but the angling was also fantastic. Certainly there were two major crises – Ulcerative Dermal Necrosis (UDN) and drift netting which led to the first Drift Net War, but by and large the whole salmon world was at its zenith.

By 1952 the abysmal catches of 1945 and 1946 were being forgotten,and modernization of equipment had really taken off. Gone was the hard graft of rowing a 26' salmon coble. Now it had a powerful outboard engine to do the job. there was no longer the back-breaking job of launching junker wheels with wooden slatted treads across 400 yds of sand with a good two tons – the coble – slung underneath. Now the wheels were pneumatic tyred, and a tractor pulled the outfit, and if there was no tractor, a petrol-driven winch hauled the three-ton load without effort.

Six men and a gurll for planting stakes and pins were out. The sand was bored by a post hole digger on the back of a Ferguson tractor, or the sand was gouged out by a high pressure pump. The donkeys and ponies that collected the salmon by ascending the cliffs had gone too, replaced by mini caterpillar tractors.

Communications were greatly improved. In 1947, I had begged Douglas Johnston to install a telephone at our River HQ at Fisherhills, Kinnaber. Scornfully, he derided the idea with, 'Young man, weren't you born with a pair of feet?' But by the early 1950s, nearly every salmon station from Aberdeen to Arbroath had its own telephone.

There is no doubt that the cold store, deep freeze complex took the stress out of daily sales of salmon to a great extent, and alleviated glut and famine; and the salmon kept coming.

Memorial to bygone prosperity: Montrose town hall.

Noël Johnston, the brother of Douglas and the latter's co-partner for many years, had died just before I joined the Company, and he left a large legacy to build a new town hall for Montrose, a much-needed public asset, and this was completed during this period.

In 1953 came the Coronation and Johnstons, now in the money, decided to celebrate in style. As the junior of the three Managing Directors, I was deputed to draw up a plan. It was arranged that the branch shop of Largs, the biggest music people in Dundee, would provide a television projector with a cinema-size screen in the newly built carpenters' shop, with hired seating for 300. Montrose's largest ballroom manager, and caterer, Tony Fortunato of the Locarno, was to provide all the food and soft drinks, and Jimmy Christieson was to provide the drinks – yes, barrels of beer, unlimited spirits and the means to drink it.

It was indeed some party! My two senior Directors made a speech of welcome to the 300 salmon fishers, wives, children of all ages, and various supporters, then disappeared. They were wise men, as were the two senior salmon fisher Superintendents who also made themselves scarce. I had no idea what I was in for, as Organizer and Bouncer in Chief, but I did manage to recruit two faithful supporters, Duncan Christie, the Foreman carpenter, and Jim Allen, a mussel worker. (Johnstons were among the largest cultivators of bait mussels in Scotland, which was a long-established subsidiary carried out in Montrose Basin.)

Actually the party was a great success; we ran out of food and we ran out of drink! Jimmy Christieson and Tony

Fortunato were towers of strength. They came to my rescue with unlimited fresh supplies, foregoing their own private celebrations. We had no major problems. Duncan and Jim helped me remove a few young drunks until they had sobered up a bit and then they were allowed back. It was all very good natured and light hearted. Then around 5 p.m. the buses provided by Johnstons took the revellers home. Those that could not walk to the buses were carried. It was an excellent 'first' in Company/employee relations.

But now back to the more serious side of Company management. At the very beginning of the 50s, other Companies were also experiencing the salmon boom. Well-known and established rivals of the Johnstons were the Powries, who held four salmon stations on lease from the Crown Commissioners between Stonehaven and Aberdeen. The leases for these stations came up for renewal in 1954 and tenders had been issued in 1952. John Stansfeld, Graham Smart and I all walked together over this section of coast, and studied form. At the end it was debated between us in America Street whether we should tender, and how much. After a long deliberation, John and Graham agreed to offer £8,500 plus rates and Salmon Fishery assessment annually which I thought was far too high, but their motion was carried, and we became the tenants. It was probably at the time the highest rent that had ever been paid for salmon fishings. Johnstons became the largest rural rate payers in Kincardineshire, surpassing all the huge landed estates of the well-heeled aristocracy!

The Powries – sons, cousins and uncles – were a formidable

clan, who had been in salmon fishing or years, and came from the Perth area. They were furious that they were to lose the tenancy, and decided to fight Johnstons tooth and nail to make them rescind their outsized bid.

The Powries first refused to hand over their shore facilities which they were entitled to do. The Crown Commissioners had never forseen this. Johnstons therefore had to build a totally new station at Portlethen, Findon and Altens, and the Crown then agreed that if and when Johnstons lost the lease, the incoming tenant would be bound to take over installations that were essential for the tenancy.

Here was the crunch. How could Johnstons build bothies, slipways, Blondin and winch sheds and access roads, all within one year? Luckily, building and planning restrictions were nil at that time for rural industry, but building materials were very much subject to licence and in short supply.

With great difficulty, John Stansfeld and Graham Smart negotiated the purchase of the necessary land, and I was given *carte blanche* to plan and build the installations. David Dundas, a Johnstons Foreman in the Montrose area, was appointed salmon Superintendent for this area, and was my Chief of Staff for the project. The Company wisely bought him a company house in Muchalls.

All through the summer and winter of 1953 we laboured – mostly in winter with salmon fishing labour when the salmon season had closed. We made concrete blocks – we bought others. An army of salmon fishers set to work. I had to acquire lorry loads of timber: what we could not utilize from the company lands at Kinnaber I bought in Aberdeen;

mostly on the black market! Roads had to be built along the cliffs. Luckily I was a skilled licensed dynamiter, and one skipper from Catterline, Harry Wyllie, then in his sixties, acted as my shotfirer's mate! At that time the situation in Ulster was peaceful. There was no limit to the amount of dynamite I bought and used!

One farmer was obstructive; maybe a friend of the Powries. He denied us access across fields to get our concrete blocks, timber and cement to a Bothy site. We drove the goods across the field one very wild, dark night and the hard frost concealed the tracks. It was done with the stealth of a wartime commando raid.

The whole operation took three months, was on a huge scale and cost thousands of pounds – hundreds of thousands by present costs – but the fact remained that we did have everything on time, a big share of the credit for which must go to David Dundas and our Mason, David Soutar of Johnshaven, a most capable lad of around 30 years old. Duncan Christie and his staff did magnificent work over the joinery requirements as did Harry Maiden and Company of Montrose over the mechanical engineering.

The Powries had declared war on us, and their next step was to prepare to remove all the shore marks which were almost essential for the correct positioning of bag nets in the sea, and these positions had been fixed over many years by trail and error. Their removal would be devastating to Johnstons.

Luckily, I had a close friend at HMS *Condor*, a naval air station at Arbroath. He was a most distinguished pilot with many decorations for his wartime exploits, and I asked him if he could photograph the whole scenario from the air. He did this with the same precision that in wartime had led to the victorious air strike on Taranto. The photos were perfect, and shown were all the salmon nets in position and the markers on shore. There was now no point in the Powries removing the markers. They tried to get the matter raised in Parliament over the misuse of naval air power but were unsuccessful. It cost me a fair contribution in salmon for the Condor wardroom mess!

That was not all. The Powries were determined to stop the men signing our bargains, the correct term for a salmon fisher's contract of employment. Every year a 'feeing market' for salmon fishers was held in Hadden Street, Aberdeen, on a day fixed in October. Hundreds of people attended, and there was no vehicular traffic. The street was quite blocked. Salmon fishers were signed on here, and contracts for thousands of pounds were negotiated by the tacksmen with rope and wire suppliers, net makers, boat builders and so forth. Most of the transactions were conducted in the two bars, and there were many drunks. John and Graham brought an attaché case stuffed with 'bargains' and currency, and were at first mistaken for snooping government inspectors, but I had been instructed to be very liberal with the drinks, and soon the alcohol was really flowing. As it took effect and we outbid the Powries, the men signed. It was a scene reminiscent of the press gangs in 1790! One man, Tom Blues of Johnshaven, would not sign. He had passed out. I had him revived with another neat whisky, he did sign, and then passed out completely! The day was done!

It cost the Company quite a lot of money and I doubt if so much was spent for years to come in the Market Arms. But it was well worth it for Johnstons!

The only blot on an otherwise prosperous landscape occurred in the spring of 1963. It was a Saturday morning in March and an easterly gale had been forecast. All the salmon nets had been slapped earlier in the week to avoid damage in this approaching storm.

I was taking things leisurely at home, this being Saturday and no net supervision required, when I received a phone call from the office, to go to Altens near Aberdeen, where there had been a serious accident at our station. Forty-five minutes later I was there. The wind howled at over 70 m.p.h., and the spume from raging seas dimmed visibility to a hundred yards. Then I discovered the extent of the accident.

Fearing that the salmon coble in Burnbanks Cove was in danger from the crashing waves, Skipper John Kenn had summoned Skipper Alex Mackie, from Nigg Bay, to get the boat higher up the slipway, when an enormous sea engulfed them both and with its backsurge carried them seawards. Luckily, a second roller threw John Kenn on to the beach, and he scrambled up the cliff path before the next roller hit, and although badly bruised, soaked to the skin, and suffering from shock and cold, he survived.

Sadly, Skipper Alex Mackie was carried seawards and drowned in the raging cauldron that was normally placid Burnbanks Cove.

It was the only serious accident that occurred in my 48 years with the Company.

12

Lapses of Security

During this period of great prosperity, 1952–77, it would be wrong to say that there were no 'hiccups'. The worst hiccup was the salmon disease UDN (Ulcerative Dermal Necrosis), which at the outset looked as if it might decimate salmon stocks as myxomatosis did with the rabbit population. To this day, and in spite of millions of pounds spent on laboratory and field research, I am doubtful if scientists really know why it came, and why it went – or at least dropped in severity. The symptoms might be compared to some extent with HIV and Aids in humans. It was not so much the disease itself that killed the salmon, but the lowering of the resistance in the fish so that they died of other causes, particularly fungus and furunculosis. The latter disease had been known for years, but UDN was something different, although records show that there had been minor plagues, possibly of the same nature, in the past century. At one time it was a very real threat to all UK salmon, but, although it seemed to hit sea trout and finnock even more than adult salmon, it passed its zenith and slowly declined.

Seals also caused great mortality of salmon at sea, not only killing salmon in the open water, but also entering salmon nets and killing and mutilating the fish entrapped therein.

Our skippers were provided with .303 rifles, later superseded by high velocity .243 rifles with telescopic sights, and reduced the menace to some extent. We were also licensed to use strychnine. We filled up dead salmon with this deadly poison and tied the salmon to head poles of bag nets which the seals were tempted to eat.

On one occasion, a dead salmon broke loose from a fly net at Boddin and was washed up at Lunan Bay, where two labrador dogs being exercised on the sand ate up part of it. Both dogs died, and the poison and its origin traced back to Johnstons and its servants. We were lucky not to be prosecuted for this terrible lapse, and compensated the owner out of court.

This dangerous practice, which had gone on for many years, was discontinued after this tragic episode.

Salmon stocks were also badly affected by river pollution, and the distilleries in Brechin were the worst offenders, which was well known to the Council representatives and officials. In those days, the effluent from whisky distillation discharged into sewers was quite lethal, as shown by the water analysis of the Public Health Department in Dundee when it was five times above the Government guideline. I was closely concerned over this as Chairman of the South Esk District Fishery Board, but the Brechin Council were afraid to act in case the distilleries were forced to close down and cause unemployment, which in turn could cause the Councillors to lose their seats!

Lapses of Security

Water abstraction from town water supplies was another problem, particularly the White Burn at Memus, much of which was the source of Forfar's water supply. The percentage that could be abstracted was set by Government statute, and the Council were required to install regulatory equipment, but this was misused in dry summers to boost the abstraction to prevent Forfar going thirsty. As a result, the burn dried up, and hundreds of parr and ova, not to mention some adult fish, died in the process.

Many a site meeting at the regulatory works I had with Forfar Council, and on one occasion, when the meeting produced the simple fact that the water abstraction was far above the permitted figure, Provost Smythe, the Council Leader, spat at me, 'Are we considering salmon before people?'

You might wonder why I was so involved in this which seems far removed from the duties of a Director of a commercial salmon fishing company. Salmon was our bread and butter, and a Director of Johnstons held the Chairmanship of the South Esk, North Esk and Bervie River Boards, in which the salmon eggs were laid, leading to what was then one of the largest rural industries in Angus and Kincardineshire.

Apart from Chairmanship of the South Esk Fishery Board, I always assumed without appointment(!) the duties of Chief of Internal Security. Few companies of any size are free of some dishonesty, and Johnstons was no exception.

Initially, I was lax with my own cash security arrangements, and around 1955 kept sums of money up to £100 in my unlocked office desk in an envelope for minor contingencies. Although the envelope was sealed, it seemed the money kept draining away, although each time I drew money I entered it on the envelope. One day I thought my writing was being forged. I laid a trap, and wrote something in German on the envelope. I found money had gone, and the forger had been unable to copy my German with his usual skill. I rang Montrose Police, who sent down that same PC Charles Johnston who had been present at the Mearns Boat Battle in 1939! There was little that Charlie didn't know about Montrose, and in no time he had arrested the culprit who duly appeared in Forfar Sheriff Court. The thief was admonished, so was I! Sheriff Ford drily observed, 'Mr Forsyth-Grant seems very careless with his money.'

The next incident concerned the annual pay-off of salmon fishers around the end of August, when the men got a settlement of their season's work, often being a four-figure sum for a single fisher. I used to distribute thousands of pounds in ready cash on this occasion, made up by the cashier in envelopes with the man's name. I took no chances on these occasions, and carried the same loaded automatic .455 pistol that I had carried in the war. (Needless to say these slap-happy arrangements were reviewed and better organized after 1977!)

To continue. The senior office staff in Johnstons were extremely busy on these settlement days, and a salmon fisher in Johnshaven said he had been paid £5 short; this seemed fair enough, and so as not to bother the busy cashier, I phoned through to Graham Smart, who was also Secretary of the Company, and asked him if he could look into the matter. I just surmised some simple mistake had been made. Then I continued with dishing out the cash at the salmon

Lapses of Security

stations of which there were many to visit between Catterline and Lunan Bay. Graham Smart had a brilliant brain and head for figures. How he figured it all out I never discovered, but on my return to the office he said he had found some serious discrepancies, and sent for the Company's auditors, then the CID. To make a long story short, the cashier was charged with embezzlement. The charges were dropped. The lady faded from the Company's employment, and a much more rigid system of bookkeeping was thereafter adopted.

By 1960 I was a busy man. John Stansfeld's health was not good, and he was off quite a lot, and often Graham Smart and I were much on our own. Besides being Joint Managing Director of Johnstons I had quite a farming empire of my own, timber interests and was prospective Parliamentary candidate for Orkney & Shetland. I had rented a suite of offices from Johnstons for my private use, and had a full-time Private Secretary and Assistant Secretary, and a part-time Political Secretary. These staff had no connection with Johnstons whatsoever, and had their own telephone and office equipment.

I shuttled between my private suite in the America Street complex and the main office of Johnstons, and, of course, was available to both interests by intercom.

One day my Secretary told me she was sure her cash box was being robbed, and she was in a terrible state about it. I told her not to worry, just to feed the cash box and note how much went missing. After a few days and the loss of some twenty pound notes, I set a trap. Both my two colleague directors who often visited my private office were away for the day – a fact well known to all our yard staff. My staff went to lunch at 1 p.m. and returned at 2.15 p.m., and I usually left at lunchtime too. There would be no one in the office for one and a quarter hours, and I made a great display of my own departure from the main office. I parked my car several hundred yards upstream from my riverside office and walked back along the dockside where no one would see me. I then entered the office block by a window, left unlocked deliberately, and got into my office without being seen, passed from it to a sub-office normally occupied by the third (Assistant) Secretary, sat down and ate my lunch. I had not long to wait, maybe twenty minutes. A knock on the office door. No reply. Another knock. Then the door quietly opened. Through the keyhole I could see a denim-covered bottom. It moved, and I heard a desk drawer open, then the clank of a cash box being opened, at which point I opened the door and walked in. A young man of the yard staff had his hand in the money box, and it was a fair cop, which fully admitted. Then he said, 'But you have no proof! Just your word against mine.' But he was the loser. Our whole conversation was being recorded on tape.

Security in my own office and the large yard premises was one thing. Security on the salmon stations stretching over 40 miles of coast and 10 miles of river was another. I did not object to salmon fishers pinching the odd fish for the pot, but I could not and would not tolerate commercial-scale and wholesale theft. I managed to track down and dismiss quite a few, but three cases are worthy of mention.

One fly net fisher, Hughie B, was a notorious thief, and being employed on a shift basis, he had little difficulty pinching a salmon or two from his fly net if the conditions were right. But he had to cross Montrose Medal Golf Course on his cycle.

My friend and hairdresser Arthur Rae was a very keen golfer, and was taking a really good tee shot when he espied a cyclist right in front of the ball! He shouted 'Fore', and the cyclist braked full and fell off his bike. Three large grilse slipped out of the sack on his back!

Another problem was a certain salmon fisher employed below the cliffs at St Cyrus, who was inclined to sell some of Johnstons' salmon, which he caught for them, to the local hostelry. My spies kept me well informed, but it was impossible to keep a watch which would give the game away and, of course, I could not employ local people for obvious reasons. I employed a detective agency in Aberdeen who posed as ordinary tourists staying at the hotel, then notorious for buying stolen salmon and game. The man was caught red handed.

The last case I will mention was of a much more serious nature. It came to my notice that one of our river skippers on night shift was stealing fish wholesale with an accomplice and I had been well informed so I informed Isaac Wright, the local Superintendent. I knew it was only a matter of time before the thief-in-chief discovered that someone was feeding me information.

One nice quiet night at sea, I was mackerel fishing off Scurdiness with Duncan Christie in his boat, and we packed up about 10 p.m. Dropping Duncan off at his house in Montrose, I motored north to my home, and a few hundred yards before I crossed the lower North Water bridge I passed

Isaac Wright walking along the road. I told him if he didn't intercept that night, I was sure thieves would know tomorrow that I was tracking their movements. This was the last chance.

I heard no more until I arrived at America Street about 10.00 a.m., and the place was swarming with police, tagging salmon in polythene sleeves and so forth. Apparently Isaac had summoned the police to a rendezvous by wireless, and the skipper and his chief accomplice were arrested, in the skipper's car as he drove from Kinnaber to Montrose.

My two colleagues were kinder hearted and less ruthless than I was, but luckily they were both in Edinburgh, so when the police asked *me* whether charges would be laid, I replied in the affirmative! After that, the case had to go ahead, which it did, and successfully, although I felt I received some reproachful looks from my colleagues. Naturally, the men were sacked on the spot.

A remarkable incident occurred about this time in my own private office, which, as I explained before, was unmanned with the front door locked at lunchtime. There was, however, a means of access for those in the know, this included Charlie Valentine, a Montrose slater who had done odd repair jobs for me for many years, and was accustomed to leaving his time sheets in my office whether it was manned or not.

When he entered the office during a lunch break he was astonished to find a stranger, who appeared American, alone in my office, and the man seemed confused by Charlie's entry. Charlie then went to Johnstons' regular workers' rest room and told my third Secretary, who was eating her lunch, what he had seen. She immediately went to the office, and found the American on the stairs, whom she recognized as US serviceman from the Edzell Navy Base, and a house tenant on my estate.

Now this man had been in the office, and had settled his rent and electricity for £175, and was due to leave for the USA two days later. He gave a poor explanation of why he had returned to the office two hours after paying his account, but said he was looking for a lavatory!

When I returned to the office at 2.30 p.m. my first Secretary was in a terrible state. Around £200 as missing from the cash box. I telephoned Montrose police, and DC Chalmers arrived in minutes. We explained the situation and he set off hot foot for Edzell Base, where he and the US security police quizzed the American. Chalmers returned to see me, and said it was quite obvious the serviceman had stolen the cash, which he had used for buying a ticket for his dog which he was flying back to the United States, but the evidence was so circumstantial that the police could not press criminal charges! I was not to be defeated, so I rang my lawyers in Stonehaven, and instructed them to take out an immediate interim interdict to prevent the American from leaving the UK until the matter was cleared up!

This was too much for the US Base, who immediately guaranteed in writing that if I dropped the matter they would reimburse me in full plus interdict costs, and this they did.

13

The First Drift Net War

The salmon netting season off the east coast of Scotland opened quite normally in February 1961, but within a week of the 'opening' there were strong rumours that the white fishers were restive, and were about to start netting red fish – something quite unknown for hundreds of years. Slowly it dawned on Johnstons that all was not well at sea. Although in the past there had been minor skirmishes with the trawlermen of Arbroath and Gourdon/Johnshaven, goodwill had always prevailed in the end over damaged gear, but this goodwill was shortly to end with a bang!

The first indication of change was when a game dealer in Letham, near Forfar, started to deal in salmon in a big way. Previously he had marketed rod-caught fish for the anglers, almost exclusively on the Kinnaird Stretch of the River South Esk, but now he was marketing sea-caught salmon. The gloves were off.

Matters came to a head when over 1,000 spring salmon, caught over a weekend, were offered for sale in Stonehaven – in our view the catchers had no right to any of the salmon they marketed.

The First Drift Net War

Our response was swift. We purchased a Dowty Turbocraft dinghy of around 15' length, with a fibreglass body and capable of speeds well exceeding 30 knots. Our purchase from the Glasgow dealers was immediate and secret, and the boat came with its own trailer.

Johnstons owned a Land Rover, and Jonathan Stansfeld and I arranged to meet the Glasgow agents at a filling station outside Forfar and transfer the trailer and boat to our Land Rover. We decided to try out the boat on Rescobie Loch, on the Montrose side of Forfar.

The launching site was deserted, other than a lone angler fishing for pike, and he told us to carry on – he had caught nothing all day. We launched the boat with the Land Rover, and did a spin round the loch. Jonathan was a most capable mechanic and had the engine going in no time, and we achieved bursts of speed of up to 25 knots. We must have cruised the loch for half an hour, frequently passing our lone angler at the launching site. By the time we had finished he had landed several pike. The propeller/aeration had put the fish on take.

Satisfied with our efforts, we made for Montrose, and immediately held a Council of War. It was agreed we would patrol off Montrose Bay that night and the crew consisted of Jonathan, myself, Isaac Wright (the North Esk Fishery Board Superintendent), and John Coull (Superintendent of Johnstons' salmon department).

It was no easy matter to get seaborne. Navigation lights were tested, so was the ex-army radio walkie-talkie and a back-up squad on land, who could follow a parallel course to the patrol boat and keep radio watch. At dusk we sailed.

Once we were a mile or so off shore in Montrose Bay the scene was chaotic. There were Gourdon and Arbroath yawls everywhere, and miles of drift nets. Luckily, the flat-bottomed Dowty with its turbo propulsion could skim over the nets, for it had no propeller, and was motivated bythe power of the water jets. The vessels we met were obviously more than curious as the what ploy our vessel was engaged in, but they were not disillusioned for long. The war had started, but apart from verbal abuse, neither side sustained casualties or damage that night. It was a first reconnaissance.

Notwithstanding, our boat was in very considerable danger: it was not really meant for night use, had very poor navigations equipment, and had not the seakeeping qualities of the enemy. If the engine failed, who would rescue us? Even the local lifeboat, crewed by local white fisherman and supporters, had already said they would not put to sea to help us. Nor did the police have anything useful to offer. We were badly outnumbered but we were determined to win.

The legal position at that time was quite clear. It was a criminal offence for anyone to take salmon at sea within one mile of low water without having legal right, and a civil offence for one mile to three miles to take salmon unless one had permission from the person(s) holding the legal right. It was not an offence to take salmon outside the three-mile limit, but this up till now had never been attempted. Further, there was confusion as to what constituted a mile – whether it was a land mile or a sea mile, and there was a difference of some 300 yards between the two. (After much research

The First Drift Net War

PATROL HOTS UP SALMON 'WAR'

Express Staff Reporter

A HIGH-SPEED white launch is "hotting up" the salmon war between fishermen and salmon fishery authorities on the East Coast.

For the launch, run by the North Esk District Fishery Board, is determined to stamp out salmon poaching by fishermen less than one mile offshore.

Fishermen say they are quite entitled to catch salmon at sea outside the limits.

The war, which started off the River Tweed, is spreading rapidly along the East Coast of Scotland.

Present focal point is off the Angus and Kincardineshire coasts.

Johnshaven fishermen have been intercepted nightly by the protection "cruiser" to find out if they are carrying salmon nets.

CHARGE

Skipper Francis McBey, of Johnshaven, was charged yesterday at Montrose harbour under the Salmon Fresh Water Protection (Scotland) Act, and gear aboard his ship, Oor Lass, was removed.

When this was done, members of Angus constabulary, directors of Messrs. Joseph Johnston and Sons, Ltd., salmon fishers, were on the jetty or aboard the craft.

Earlier yesterday Mr. Forsyth Grant, of the North Esk Board, said:

"Unless we take some action to try to curb this suspected poaching, we'll not have a salmon left in the North Esk in a few years' time.

"All salmon net owners and river proprietors along the East Coast are seriously worried about the way in which salmon are being caught offshore regardless of consequences."

Owners of fishings on the rivers Tay and South Esk have been complaining recently of a new threat from the "Nylon Curtain" boats which, by using hanging nets off the river mouths, have been landing large hauls of salmon.

Landing their catches usually about 6.30 a.m. in Arbroath, the nylon net boats sent one-and-a-quarter tons of fish to London on Tuesday.

DEPLETION

Two boats fishing off Montrose have each been catching 50 salmon a day. Proprietors say this off-shore fishing is bound to lead to depletion of salmon stocks in the river.

Now they allege that the nylon boats, by constructing and using a smaller mesh net, are also starting to catch trout.

The River Fisheries Boards are powerless to prevent the nylon curtain being drawn across their river outlets—their powers extend only 500 yards below the low-water mark.

And the Scottish Secretary has told protesting proprietors that he can only inerfere if they show proof of having suffered loss.

and legal argument by the end of 1961 it was fixed at sea miles, not land miles.)

An inconclusive duel started in our first patrol week, with *Oor Lass* of Johnshaven, about 1½ miles off the harbour, and although the exchange was only verbal, it made history in the press, and drew a lot of publicity. Next was the fierce confrontation with the Gourdon boat *Silver Fern* (Skipper, James Cargill). This boat was intercepted in Montrose Bay with nets down within one mile off the shore. The boat was challenged, but refused to stop. Instead it passed the speedboat as if to ram. The speedboat saw the *Silver Fern* off. Apart from having a top speed of four times that of *Silver Fern*, it had a much tighter turning circle, and could run over the nets with impunity. The battle lasted nearly an hour, and ended with *Silver Fern* trying to ram the speedboat on the other side of the drift net, whereupon the drift net fouled the *Silver Fern*'s propeller and the boat was totally immobilized! Having taken the name and number of *Silver Fern* the patrol boat proceeded back to Montrose and a conference was held with the Clerk of the South Esk Fishery Board, Solicitor Mr Stanley Scott Robinson, MBE, later to become Sheriff Scott Robinson of Inverness.

The crew on this occasion had been Jonathan Stansfeld, myself (also Chairman of the South Esk Fishery Board) and Superintendent Donald MacIntyre of the South Esk Board. It was agreed that Donald should go to Gourdon and shadow the *Silver Fern*, now under tow, to the harbour, and charge the skipper and crew with a criminal offence. By 5.00 a.m., *Silver Fern* was about 2 miles off Gourdon, and Donald and

The First Drift Net War

The Press and Journal

TUESDAY JUNE 20 1961

1. MEARNS FISHERMEN IN NEW INCIDENT
2. MINISTRY 'SOLVES' SKY RIDDLE
3. RECEPTIONS: GUESTS AND HOTEL STAFF QUIZZED

THE SALMON WAR FLARES

Fishers jeer as Gourdon nets are taken

A TOP official of the Firth of Forth Fishermen's Association is expected at Gourdon to-day to investigate a series of alleged incidents in the salmon fishing "war" off the Kincardine coast.

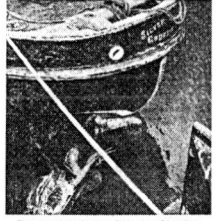

Latest of the incidents was the seizure by police and water bailiffs yesterday of the nets of the Gourdon fishing boat, Silver Fern, which is skippered by Mr James Cargill.

A crowd of about fifty fishermen and their womenfolk jeered the police and bailiffs as they took the nets from the Silver Fern at Gourdon early yesterday morning.

And Skipper Cargill said last night: "If it had happened later in the morning, when more of the fishermen were about, there would have been a riot."

He alleged that his net had been cut by a launch employed by the North Esk District Salmon Fishery Board off St Cyrus. But Mr R. Scott Robinson, clerk to the Board, denied that the net was cut by the launch.

"We say had to wait until the vessel came into port where the net was taken into custody by officers," said Mr Robinson, "and the man was charged with a contravention of the Salmon Fisheries Protection Act."

Whatever the outcome of this latest case, fishermen's feelings along the Kincardine coast are certainly running high. Said Mr Leslie Davidson, skipper of the Margarita, which towed the Silver Fern to port yesterday after a net fouled her propeller: "We have our differences here but in this kind of thing you have to stand together."

This ferling away, Mr Norman C. Osborne, secretary of the Firth of Forth Fishermen's Association, who is expected at Gourdon to-day to meet Mr James Stewart, secretary of Gourdon Fishermen's Association.

The association Gourdon took are affiliated to the Firth of Forth Association, which embraces eight such associations in fishing communities from Stonehaven to Eyemouth.

'LIMIT BID'

Mr Stewart said last night: "I something to be done for the fishermen, it will be done by the Firth of Forth Association." Mr Osborne was out here to-day, but he was expecting to see everything being done, but he said up. He will certainly take a lead on here."

Background to yesterday's incident is that angry fishermen of Gourdon and Johnshaven feel they are entitled to fish for salmon as long as they have but now than a crew from the shore. But they allege that several incidents involving the launch recently acquired by the North Esk Board show that an attempt is being made to impose a three-mile limit.

The Board have replied that at certain times it might be an offence to fish for salmon within the three-mile limit and at other times a could be said by the proprietors or tenants of coastal salmon fisheries.

NET WAIT

After describing the alleged net-cutting and the fouling of his propeller by part of his net, Skipper Cargill said he had got in touch with a solicitor with a view to charging the Board with the expenses of a new net. If he could get a loan of another fisherman's net he might be back fishing next week. Otherwise he did not know how long it would be before he could resume fishing. "I had to wait five weeks to twenty the nets I have just out from the time I ordered them," he said.

And he forecast that drift-net fishing for salmon was the coming thing. "Most of the fishermen here are getting the idea," he said.

Mr Robinson, for the Board, described Skipper Cargill as a legal who was calling an offence.

I watched her from the top of the brae. I telephoned Inverbervie police with an update of the position, and asked them to be present, after which we proceeded to the harbour. There was no one about, but within minutes the news got round, probably passed by ship's radio to the shore supporters.

As the *Silver Fern* entered harbour under tow, over 200 supporters, jeering and threatening Donald and me, began to converge on us. The police were powerless to intervene; and when Donald and I got into my car to avoid missiles which were now coming, the crowd rushed the police and tried to push the car into the harbour. It was a real riot. The police told me to drive off, and pushed the crowd aside, and I managed to get through the crowd and volley of missiles and escape up the hill, known as Brae Road. Later, the complaint was served on skipper James Cargill without a second riot taking place. At the trial that followed, the claim by *Silver Fern* that the speedboat had cut the drift nets was rubbished – too late the defence discovered that the speedboat had no propeller.

Many battles were to follow, and one of the hottest was the interception of the yawl *Bairn's Pride* of Arbroath, off the Red Head of Angus, by the speedboat. Having ordered *Bairn's Pride* to make for Arbroath, I wirelessed Superintendent Miller of the Tay Fisheries Board, in whose area the offence had been committed, and asked him to meet us at Arbroath Harbour.

On arrival in Arbroath, *Bairn's Pride* secured to a jetty and so did we just round the corner. A jeering crowd of white fisher supporters was held in good check by a powerful

The First Drift Net War

presence of police. Notwithstanding the crowd was able to direct volleys of spittle at Jonathan and myself below in the speedboat until I clambered to the pier head, defended by the police. Up a ladder came a *Bairn's Pride* crew member carrying a chart, which I asked the police to confiscate. The crew man made a run for it, over bridge and through the harbour but a constable and I caught him, and he was forced back to the pier head with the chart.

At the trial in Forfar, David Swankie and his crew were found guilty and suitably fined. He tried to prove that in his navigation he was outside the mile limit with his drift nets, but with the expertise I had gathered from my own court martial for a navigation offence in the Navy in 1944, I was able to rubbish everything he said. Whether the truth was twisted or not on this occasion I could not possibly comment! Point made is that the case was won.

Many other cases were heard and disposed of in action with the speedboat, but one is worthy of special mention: when skipper William Harvey of Johnshaven, the fishing boat *Fruitful* and crewman Frederick Burnett of Johnshaven were charged with an offence off Rockall in St Cyrus Bay.

Willie Harvey was an old friend of mine. He had been employed by me as a deer-stalking ponyman at Ullapool seven years before I intercepted his boat off Rockall, but I could not withdraw the prosecution just because he was an old friend. In his defence he claimed he was not fishing for salmon, but for cod, and in this he was supported by venerable arch enemy of Johnstons, Richard Davidson (Dick) McBay, a 76-year-old Chief of the McBay clan. Not even Dick's evidence saved Willie Harvey and Fred Burnett. They were suitably fined.

The most intensive drift netting for salmon occurred off the Angus/Kincardineshire coast, but had escalated all over East Scotland, from Wick in the north, to Berwick in the south. Salmon anglers and legal netsman alike saw the end of salmon on the horizon and at a meeting of Salmon Fishery Boards in Aberdeen it was agreed that the Don, Dee, Bervie, North Esk, South Esk, Tay and Tweed would combine as allies to fight the drift net fishermen. As Johnstons had been the first and only company so far to battle with the drift netters at sea, they were asked to operate a combined anti-poacher operation and I was placed in charge of their sea operations.

Quite obviously the speedboat was inadequate to operate off Fraserburgh or Berwick without land back-up, and the operation of the speedboat even in the Montrose area at night – the zero time for drift netting – was a perilous risk.

I was given permission to buy a diesel drifter of 70 to 80 ft, with good sea-keeping qualities, and a crew. I enlisted the help of Lieut.-Com. Robert Young, with whom I served in the Navy, and who was now Managing Director of Jones Buckie Slip, one of the foremost builders of fishing boats in Scotland. I examined a number of boats that were for sale, amongst them *Dundarg*, FR121, which had been my first command in the Navy in 1940. In spite of the nostalgic connection, I settled on *Souvenir*, a motor drifter with a Buckie crew, and in no time Johnstons became the owner of this vessel.

The First Drift Net War

Now we could keep at sea in any condition that the east coast fishing fleet could utilize, for at this time no craft of over 50-foot length was being used.

These anti drift net operations were taking up so much of my time that I was neglecting the inshore operations of Johnstons, and I sought an understudy which was speedily approved. Through the Admiralty Employment Board I engaged Lieut.-Com. Brothers, RN, who was just about to retire from the Navy at Rosyth.

Sadly, I found that although Brothers was quite good at victualling the *Souvenir* and attending to administration matters which were very considerable, he lacked the offensive spirit to go out and attack the drift netters on the high seas.

The skipper and crew of *Souvenir* whom we had taken over were very competent at handling their ship, but were uneasy when it came to confrontation and showers of verbal abuse from their kith and kin, so in fact the employment of Lieut.-Com. Brothers was not the success I had expected. In practice it was useless to fly my flag in harbour, and I had to be afloat!

I intercepted drift netters from the Pentland Firth to the Farne Islands, and there were too many prosecutions to list here. When I was in the speedboat no other member of crew was qualified in any sort of navigation other than myself, and as a witness had to be corroborated, the position was tricky in the extreme. I had to rely on landsmen's memories in finding transits on land to fix our position at sea, and this could be corroborated for a 'fix' by the compass adjuster of Aberdeen. Now in *Souvenir* I had plenty back-up for navigational accuracy in Lieut.-Com. Brothers, besides the skipper and mate of *Souvenir*. Whereas in the speedboat it was extremely dangerous to sail with the wind exceeding Force 3, and with visibility of under 4 miles, in *Souvenir* I could operate in Force 7 and in dense fog, due to the Decca navigator and other electronic aids.

Souvenir had a top speed of 10 knots, and the drift netters from north to south kept a check on her position, whether she was at sea, or in port, at Montrose or Aberdeen. Their spies radioed the drift netters using the code name they called *Souvenir* – Yogi Bear. Often I listened in to their broadcasts on *Souvenir*'s radio. I found the best way to confuse our enemies was to stand well out to sea, any 15 miles from shore, and then pounce on the drift net fleet from seaward when they had their nets down and either they fled empty handed, and we retained the nets, or they risked confrontation and likely prosecution. We took a good many boats in this way, but for me it was very time consuming. I could not stand 24 hours offshore and supervize legal salmon fishing or our own off the Kincadineshire Angus coast.

I was at home one evening in dense fog, and *Souvenir* was alongside the jetty in Aberdeen. I thought this might be the perfect night to surprise the Gourdon fleet who would not expect *Souvenir* to put to sea in dense fog.

I managed to contact the *Souvenir* skipper by phone, and told him to prepare for sea in 90 minutes, and then I motored to Aberdeen and boarded. We cleared Aberdeen Harbour almost immediately and steamed in dense fog, using electronic aids, to a position ten miles off shore off Tod Head Lighthouse,

The First Drift Net War

just south of Stonehaven. By 2.00 a.m. the fog thinned, and I reckoned the Gourdon Fleet would be tempted to leave port, and when we arrived off the coast at 3.30 a.m., the fleet was at sea, with many drift nets down. They were all fishing without lights, except for the 'winkies' at the extremity of the drift nets, and conditions were ideal for collisions.

Out of the wisps of fog, *Souvenir* emerged, just as a drift netter heaved a dan buoy overboard to mark his net. He was steaming without lights, and we began to chase him. Probably he had electronic navigational aids too, for we zigzagged on the chase for over an hour, always returning to his original position or near it – the floating drifting net. He was not quite sure of our identity and after a time I hailed the boat. 'It's a cold night,' said I, 'just the time for a tot of rum!' We were almost alongside the boat at this time, and two crew members of the boat could make me out in the dim light of our navigation lights which were on. I was holding a bottle of rum. 'Would you like some?' I shouted. They replied in the affirmative, and when we were virtually alongside I threw over the bottle of rum which they caught.

The drift net boats used to cover their numbers to avoid identification, but within seconds of the boats exchanging the rum, I flashed on all our lights, and the boat that had shot the drift net was clearly identified, number and all. They were duly booked, charged and later prosecuted. The boat was owned and operated by the Morrison Brothers of Gourdon, who were first-class white sea fishermen, and their boat had been newly built. Several years after, I met skipper Morrison in a pub in Montrose by accident and we discussed the incident. Good naturedly he told me it was the most expensive tot of rum he had ever consumed.

As I have said, *Souvenir* patrolled from Wick to the Farne Islands, and we instigated many prosecutions and worked very closely with Colonel Michael Ryan, Chief of the River Tweed Commissioners security team.

All the Fishery Boards concerned in this operation were most co-operative through their Chief Executives and financed the costly operation of *Souvenir* without demur. I was most grateful to them.

We won this battle after two years, in spite of the supine lack of support from the Department of Agriculture and Fisheries in Edinburgh in general, and the Chief Inspector of Salmon Fisheries in particular. These civil servants who also controlled the fishery cruisers, were as supportive as dying cod!

I think I am right in saying that the Secretary of State for Scotland, Jack MacLeay, (later created Viscount Muirshiel) took fright, expecting that this civil war at sea could lead to loss of life, and he succeeded in pushing through a 'Statutory Instrument' effectively banning drift netting for salmon in coastal waters. Temporarily the first Drift Net War had ended. The cost was very considerable. *Souvenir* was sold, and the crew retired. So was Lieut.-Com. Brothers. For a period at least the old established means of salmon fishing continued without hassle. The drift netters of Gourdon and Arbroath withdrew to lick their wounds. Their bitterness was intense. My name, once quite popular in Gourdon amongst the white fishers with whom I had associated in 1939, was the most hated in the village. Several years later, I was drinking quietly in the Gourdon Pub when the owner eyed me evilly. 'Michael Grant,' he said. 'You're no welcome here.' He was right!

So this era had passed. I went back to full-time occupation in Johnstons as Director of the Coastal Fishings. In spite of the cost of fighting this, the first Drift Net War, Johnstons were now doing well. We were still in the golden era.

AS THE SALMON WAR COMBATANTS DISCUSS THEIR OFF-SHORE CLASH

'Captain Kidd' speaks out

By COLIN SMITH

LIEUT.-COMMANDER MICHAEL FORSYTH-GRANT, swashbuckling captain of a "private navy" fighting a salmon war with East Coast fishermen, said yesterday:

"I am being painted the villain of the piece—a sort of 20th-century Captain Kidd—and it's all very distressing."

An ex-wartime motor torpedo boat commander, he now leads his two-ship navy in dawn swoops against fishermen using expensive nylon nets to take salmon illegally inside the one mile limit.

But yesterday Lieut.-Commander Forsyth-Grant—a director of Messrs. J. Johnston and Sons, Montrose salmon fishers, and a member of the North Esk Fishery Board — denied allegations by fishermen that his patrol boats were destroying their £1,000 nets.

He said: "Nets are cut by propellers but I assure you it is not done intentionally. Sometimes it is quite dark and impossible to pick out the small cork floats. We would not damage fishermen's property.

'Captain Kidd'— runs the private navy

"After all we are not pirates. We don't use grappling irons and we don't have cutlass-waving boarding parties either."

The Forsyth-Grant private navy consists of a turbo-jet no-propeller speedboat (to avoid damaging nets) and a 70-foot seine/netter, the Souvenir.

14

Some Angling Feats and Misadventures

Up to 1938, I think I was a very keen angler, and was much encouraged by my father, and a friend of my mother's: Colonel Renny Tailyour rented Dun water on the River South Esk now part of the National Trust at Dun House, which was a reasonable salmon water, a good sea trout water, and superlative for finnock. The bottom of the water was tidal, the high water infilling the lower stretches of the South Esk above the Turnpike Bridge. I started sea trout fishing here in April 1935, and had no waders. I fished all day up to my thighs in cold melting snow water and had flu for the last ten days of my school holidays, but it did not put me off. Next holidays, I acquired a pair of waders as a gift from my sister's latest 'catch'! Over the next few years, under the Colonel's good guidance, I became fairly proficient at wet fly fishing for trout and finnock. One evening, I was fishing through the dusk on a Saturday night while my long-suffering father sat and watched me from the bank. He had to attend as he was my chauffeur, and just a few minutes to

Some Angling Feats and Misadventures

midnight he called on me to finish, as the weekly close time was about to start. I called back, 'Wait a few minutes. No one will be watching us!' Luckily he was furious, and I waded ashore to join him, and we crossed the river by the main Aberdeen–Glasgow railway line viaduct, watching out for trains. Sitting on a parapet of the viaduct in the gloom, were two river watchers – obviously waiting for us to break the law. It was lucky that my father was a firm disciplinarian.

Up to 1936, I had little chance to catch salmon, and was delighted when in April of that year I was invited by my chum Roger Burnett to stay with him and his august parents in Crathes Castle, Banchory, and fish for salmon. The Burnett family, one of the oldest in Scotland, owned the best beats of the famous Aberdeen Dee at that time, the most famous of which were Cairnton and Wood End. However, they retained Lower Crathes in their own hands, and here, with two ghillies in attendance, Roger and I, with the Chairman of Britain's largest asbestos company who was also a house guest, got down to serious salmon fishing.

My tackle was very ancient, belonging to a deceased uncle, and had been neglected in store for thirty years. It was 17' green heart rod with splicings (no suction joints) and was very heavy. Roger was an excellent Spey caster, but I was a complete novice, and spent most of the time catching bushes and trees behind me, or letting a great mass of line splash into the water just off my rod tip. I asked Roger to change places, as he was following me, and seemed to have little chance while I disturbed the water so disgracefully. So we changed places, and I was able to watch Roger's superb action, and learn a little myself. He was using a fly called an Akroyd, and I was using a Mar Lodge – very big fly, just over 2 inches in length.

By 11.30 none of the three of us had touched a salmon, but shortly afterwards a salmon took me twenty yards behind Roger. It rushed into midstream and the reel screamed. Downstream it went, and Roger reeled in and fled the riverside as I hoofed it downstream, fearful that I would lose all my line. Another ten yards and I would run no more. There were overhanging willows, and the water was 6 ft deep sheer below them so I could not continue further downstream. The ghillie, who had been shouting the most confusing instructions, grunted, 'Ye'll lose him. Ye can gang nae further.' I don't think that the salmon heard him, for it suddenly reversed course, and started boring upstream at full speed while I frantically reeled in the lost line. After twenty minutes, the 10 lb spring fish lay dead on the bank – my first salmon, and the only fish caught that day on the beat.

Major General Sir James Burnett of Leys, Roger's father, was a fearsome figure. He ruled his family with a rod of iron, and that included guests. Breakfast was sharp at 8.30 a.m., normally grilled salmon, and anglers were marched to the river at 9.30 a.m. There was to be no slacking, nor stand easy, and no tea breaks. You fished until 1 p.m. whether you liked it or not. Then you had a fair lunch break with salmon sandwiches. There was a stand easy at 4 p.m. and you resumed fishing until 6 p.m. Then it was march back to the Castle and change for dinner. I occupied a room in a stone turret; no wallpaper nor conveniences but I think it did have an electric light.

Some Angling Feats and Misadventures

Dinner was at 8 p.m. Dinner jackets to be worn. Youths of fifteen were expected to be seen but not heard. The main course was salmon. After dinner, the older generation retired to the drawing room and billiard room, but Roger and I were allowed to go into Aberdeen to the cinema, driven by Rohays, Roger's sister – one of the most beautiful teenagers I was ever to set eyes on. (She later became Lady Boyd Rochfort, married to the Queen's trainer, and sired Henry Cecil, top Newmarket trainer.)

Salmon angling: the author in the 1970s.

I stayed at Crathes three days, with the daily rota the same. Neither Roger nor I caught another fish. I have a horrid feeling that it really cured me of my fanatical lust to fish for salmon. Notwithstanding, it was a wonderful experience and, with the landing of my first salmon, one I shall never forget.

Over the next fifty years, I landed over a thousand salmon in the North Esk alone, and at that time was probably the angler with the highest score of the North Esk salmon then living, but it was not skill that gave me that distinction – it was due to enjoying the best spring salmon fishing in the

A Salmon Fisher Remembers

United Kingdom, free of charge, for all those years. I shall not bore the reader with repetitions of the salmon I caught, but will record the feats of others.

During the period 1950–65 the Kinnaber stretch of the River North Esk had probably the best finnock fishing in the United Kingdom. I would rate it higher than Bridge of Dun on the South Esk, and better than the Ythan estuary. The record single day catch for an angler at Dun was 99. Although the angler tried desperately for his 100, he never made it. The record stood for many years.

Netting stopped on the North Esk on 31 August, and the finnock gathered in shoals in the lower reaches. Although Johnstons let the angling of Morphie down to the Bridge Pool – the edge of tidal water – the Kinnaber stretch from the Bridge Pool to the sea was retained for the Directors and their friends, with a resident ghillie to assist them, one Roland Milne, whose family name was a byword to all fishers – rod and net – on the North Esk. He lived in a cottage in the centre of the beat.

I was still keen on finnock fishing, and was often accompanied by friends one of whom was Charlie Valentine, a Montrose slater by trade, and a well-known character, previously mentioned in this book. He had a day off from his work and so had I, but I could not accompany him to fish as I was grouse shooting on the hills. So I gave Charlie *carte blanche* to fish on his own.

Charlie killed 137 finnock that day! It was an all-time record which few people would achieve in a whole season. Fellow angers were disgusted when they heard that Charlie

Some Angling Feats and Misadventures

Charlie Valentine at the pondage pool.

had sold his catch around hotels of Montrose, but come to think of it, it was probably no worse than all the salmon we netted and sold in London.

Charlie Valentine was also with me one memorable day at Morphie Dyke around 1950, on the 'Opening Day'. Major Foster and his wife from the famous Park Fishings on the Aberdeen Dee had been invited to fish by my colleagues, so the Major and his wife, with head ghillie and foreman Roland Milne, took the South Bank (Angus) and Charlie and I took

James Harrington's red-letter day: 11 salmon in 3 hours.

Bill Gilbert.

Some Angling Feats and Misadventures

the North (Kincardineshire). It was an atrociously cold day, with intermittent snow and icy wind. The line kept freezing in the ferules of our rods, and frequently had to be broken off, or the line would just not go out. We started at 1 p.m. and it was drk by 4.15 p.m. By that time, we had landed 36 salmon. That record stood for 40 years.

Another remarkable feat was that of James Harrington, a friend of mine from Walton on Thames, who had plenty of experience coarse fishing, but had very little chance of salmon fishing at that time. I asked my own ghillie/gamekeeper to accompany him, and showed them the Morphie Stretch at 10.00 a.m. I told them I had to work in Montrose, but would be out with a picnic lunch at 1 p.m. When I arrived, James had 13 salmon on the bank to which he added another three in the afternoon.

James had prospered well in his engineering business and since then has rented some excellent beats on other rivers, but this record is one he has never beaten – nor will!

Bill Gilbert was a Merchant Navy engineer officer and one of the real characters of Montrose. He was a keen fisherman, but no believer in Queensberry rules.

The Chief of Staff of one of Lord Inchcape's many companies was staying in the Park Hotel at Montrose and, as I was an old friend of his wife, asked if I could fix some salmon angling for him. All I could offer was the Morphie Stretch of the North Esk which, although netted, offered superb sport when the nets were not operating. I could not offer him a ghillie, so I asked Bill Gilbert if he would oblige. Both the tycoon and Bill fished all day without luck and were just about to pack up when Bill asked his guest if he would like the feel of playing a fish, to which the guest, quite unsuspecting, replied in the affirmative.

Within a minute, Bill, a master in the art, had sniggered a large salmon, and handed the rod to the guest. The guest had a wonderful run of the fish for nearly twenty minutes, and the fish was coming nicely to the bank. Bill was about to land it, when he suddenly removed the cigarette which was perpetually drooping from his mouth, and touched the taut line. Bingo – and the fish had gone.

The guest was luckily lost for words. When he turned about to recover from his shock and horror, he was staring into the face of the Head Baillie of the river. Bill had seen him coming just in time. In spite of the disaster, the tycoon enjoyed his day intensely and they recounted their experience over drinks at the bar of the Park Hotel that evening. I did think our guest was behaving out of character but I didn't realize that he and Bill had consumed one bottle of whisky that day, and were into another. For the second time that day, the tycoon whirled around to get his bearings. He did not find them, but fell to the floor totally intoxicated. With some embarrassment, I carried him to his bedroom assisted by the owner of the hotel with some assistance from Bill.

By the early eighties, the spring fishing of the North Esk had dwindled away, and I considered that it would be more profitable not to net the Morphie Dyke beat, but to let it for angling. My two colleagues agreed to this, for a trial period of six weeks, but the problem was to provide a ghillie. Johnstons' men were all heavily committed to net fishing,

Some Angling Feats and Misadventures

Ken Adam: a very celebrated game-keeper and ghillie.

and in any case the ordinary salmon fisher was not mentally suited to ghillieing, not being 'gentlemen's gentlemen'. I therefore suggested my own gamekeeper, Ken Adam, who was both an excellent low ground keeper, and a first-class salmon ghillie. He could be spared from mid-February to the first of April, before pheasant rearing started.

The angling quickly got under way. At a rent of £4,000 a week, for six rods, it was a better return than could be had from netting. There was no shortage of takers, and this was the beginning of the Morphie salmon angling beat, one of the most productive in all Scotland.

Having two jobs was really too much for Ken, and he started to train a young salmon fisher as a professional ghillie, and after a year or two Peter Winder became a most competent full-time ghillie and Ken retired.

Notwithstanding, Ken ghillied for me now and again, and one day we invited one Andy Hill, a daredevil ex-Fleet air arm pilot who had his own airline at Aberdeen. He was a very keen angler, but had a streak of Bill Gilbert in him.

I had only two pools in which I could fish, the Batts and

Allan's Stream, because upstream of this, the Morphie beat was let to millionaires. I explained this to Andy, and told him he must not go or fish upstream of the top pool. Ken and I went for a bar lunch at the neighbouring Hillside Hotel, but Andy wanted to fish through our lunch hour, so we left him.

On our return we could see no sign of him, but his car was still there. I was very worried, and while I was thinking of phoning the police, as I thought he could have fallen in, he appeared from 'nowhere' upstream, much to my relief. Shortly afterwards I left for the office, neither Ken nor I having caught a thing.

Later Andy told Ken that he had 'poached' two salmon from an upstream pool while we lunched and had hidden under a bush while a millionaire's car passed by. I was very unwilling to renew my invitation!

Shortly before my retirement from Johnstons in 1986, Colonel Jack Woodroffe invited me to fish on the prestigious Upper Kinnaird Water on the South Esk. I told Jack that I was not really an angler, but would much appreciate a liquid lunch with him at the fishing lodge. I imagined there would only be the two of us. I mentioned this to Ken Adam, and he asked if he could ghillie for me. I said I would only be staying an hour or so as I had work to do in the office, and he said he would meet me at the fishing lodge at 2 p.m.

I arrived at 12.45 p.m. at the lodge in my very ordinary office clothes and no waders, when to my horror I discovered Jack had invited a whole lot of VIPs. The Lord Lieutenant, Lord Dalhousie, the President of the Fly Fishers' Club, and

Some Angling Feats and Misadventures

the Chairman of the London Stock Exchange! I looked like a down and out tramp, but my ego was lifted by the immaculate Ken in a plus-fours suit who put me to shame in my well-stained Bedford Cord slacks and dirty tweed coat!

The distinguished party had fished without any success all morning, and the river was very high after a night of heavy rain. Jack accompanied me to the Dyke Pool, but I could not fish it, as it required thigh waders, and I had not brought mine. I asked him to fish it while I watched. He had no success.

However, the pool down below was fishable from the bank without waders, so I started to spin with a 2" wooden minnow. Ken, an expert angler, told me to let my minnow come over the top of a single boulder and let it hang in the backwater for a second or two. I botched the first cast, but my second was perfect. The slack of the line tautened and a fish had taken – then the line went limp. 'Fuck it,' I cried, and whipped the point upwards. Lo and behold, the salmon was still on!

It played like a demon and there was no shortage of spectators. 'You've caught it by the tail,' shouted a Dundee Courier correspondent across the water. 'Rubbish,' cried Ken, 'how could you possibly foul hook a fish with a swollen river like this?' I played the fish oblivious to all comments, and after fifteen minutes drew it quietly to the bank. To my amazement, Ken discarded his net and handled the fish to his bosom and then flicked it on to the bank, where he quickly despatched it, to the hearty applause of all present – the only salmon caught that day. I was very chuffed with my success. I had shown that I did catch salmon by rod and line as well as net.

It was not until later that Ken told me the fish was foul hooked and that was why it played so well. The salmon had spat out the minnow, but had been re-hooked when I whipped the point of the rod, catching its tail. Ken had landed the fish in such an unusual way to conceal how it was caught.

It was several years before I dared to tell the true story, and it raised a lot of mirth.

15

The Second Drift War

The first Drift Net War had virtually ended by the end of 1964, and apart from small sporadic raids from Johnshaven, the coastal salmon fisheries remained fairly quiet for the next thirteen years. The splendid co-operation of the Salmon Fishery Boards from the Dee in Aberdeen to the Tweed at Berwick in financing the patrol boat *Souvenir* really led to the elimination of large inshore drift netting operations. Johnstons had also sold the Dowty Turbocraft, and neither the Fishery Boards nor the legal coastal net operators had anything for patrolling their waters. The ban on drift net fishing in territorial water was initially a stern deterrent to the drift netters, but as time went by the ineptitude of St Andrews House in general and the Inspectorate of Salmon Fisheries for Scotland in particular was noted by fishermen further south than Arbroath. Few of the Arbroath or Gourdon drift netters had boats larger than 48 ft but it was now the turn of the Firth of Forth fishermen with boats around 70 ft that entered the second war, with Dunbar and Port Seton (Cockenzie) leading the offensive.

Neither the civilian-manned Fishery Cruisers nor the Navy-manned Fishery Protection Squadron appeared to have any clear instructions to prosecute drift netting, and some of the police and fishery officers were on the side of the white, turned red, fishermen. During the period of the second Drift Net War, at least two policemen were drowned and another transferred while involved in illegal netting or leaking information to those involved. Nor were the local fishery officers guiltless on giving advice and aid to those engaged in this practice. The police tried desperately to keep out of the confrontation, and more than one Procurator Fiscal showed total ignorance of the salmon fishery laws and failed to proceed under the proper statues. It was under a very difficult situation that the second Drift Net War exploded in 1976.

Johnstons were aware of the 'gathering storm' by their own sources of intelligence and it was well that they were

The war at sea: speedboat *Trafalgar*.

prepared. Noel Smart had purchased a Dell Quay Dory about 15 ft overall, with two outboard 65 hp motors. It was capable of a speed of around 35 knots, and came with a transport and launching trailer. The speedboat was christened *Trafalgar*.

On 23 August 1976 Noel Smart telephoned me to say that a large fleet of drift netters were operating in Lunan Bay. He had alerted Alec Coull our Foreman mechanic, responsible for the speedboat, and was having the boat launched at Rossie Island, Montrose. He had also requested police presence, and that of Superintendent MacIntyre of the South Esk District Salmon Fishery Board.

When I arrived from home seven miles away, the scrambling of boat crew, River Superintendent and two police officers in uniform aboard had gone without a hitch, and within minutes we were heading down Montrose Harbour and Girdleness at 35 knots. Still running at full speed past Usan we entered Lunan Bay, and there was a sight that Sir Richard Grenville must have witnessed with his little *Revenge* against the Spanish 53!

The Bay was choc-a-block with big, 70 ft drift netters and we attacked the first who was beginning to haul his drift nets. This was the *Rosehaugh* of Port Seton skippered by William Flockhart Thomson.

Mechanic Alec Coull manoeuvred *Trafalgar* alongside *Rosehaugh* and the two police, Donald MacIntyre and I boarded without opposition and were actually on board before were even noticed, so involved were the crew in hauling their drift net. Salmon aplenty were coming on board with the net.

I produced my warrant card to Thomson and told him I had reason to believe he was committing a criminal offence by drift netting in a forbidden area, and asked him to finish hauling his net and proceed to Montrose. He was most abusive.

The drift net was hauled aboard with around forty salmon and I ordered Thomson to sail for Montrose, which he refused to do, and he set off seawards. The other members of the illegal fleet had witnessed the commotion and had concentrated together a mile or so seaward for a powwow.

I asked the police to arrest the skipper, and I would take the boat to Montrose. I had already asked Alec Coull to take *Trafalgar* to port, and alert the authorities as to what was going on. The two policemen were indeed 'out of their depth'. Not unnaturally they had never been in a situation like this before; in fact I doubt if they had been to sea before.

They demurred about arresting Thomson, whom, I suggested, they should handcuff to the mast, and really played no further part other than as witnesses. Their radio could not reach ashore to get instructions.

Rosehaugh joined the powwow, and MacIntyre and I were showered with abuse, including suggestions that we should be thrown overboard. After this, Thomson left the fleet and steered further from the coast and started to dump all the salmon. I duly cautioned him against doing this in the presence of the police.

After an hour or so of steaming around. Thomson seemed to realize the gravity of the offence, and sailed for Montrose, where he was arrested with all his crew with a mighty police presence (for Montrose!).

The Second Drift War

Daily Record 5th March 77

STATEMENT OF ACCOUNT

To destroying 29 salmon £2500

To hi-jacking two policemen £50

TOTAL: £2550

(Payment in full within four months or further action will be taken)

Forsyth-Grant   Donald McIntyre   PC Bell   PC Powell

Skipper William Thomson

Skipper pays bill for wild day out

THE skipper who shanghaied a boarding party netted a huge fine yesterday.

William Thomson was fined £50 for hijacking four people—including two policemen.

And he must pay a further £2500 for destroying evidence—29 salmon.

Outside the court at Arbroath, the 28-year-old fisherman from Port Seton, East Lothian, said: "I don't think I'll be back in these waters again."

A third charge of illegal fishing within the one mile of low water mark off the Angus coast was found not proven.

During a three-day trial, the jury heard of hijinks at sea involving boarding parties and salty language off the coast at Lunan Bay, near Arbroath.

A boarding party led by former Naval Lieutenant Commander Michael Forsyth-Grant, and including water bailiff Donald McIntyre and PC Howard Powell and Charles Bell, had gone aboard Thomson's Leith-registered fishing boat Rosehaugh to probe illegal fishing.

But when the boarding party demanded that the 50ft. fishing boat should head back to port they were threatened with being thrown into the sea.

The court heard it was almost two hours later before the vessel headed back.

CAUGHT

In evidence yesterday, Thomson, part-owner of the Rosehaugh, claimed they had been fishing OUTSIDE the limit when a speedboat drew alongside.

He admitted that he had accidentally caught salmon earlier, but the fish were thrown overboard.

Thomson claimed Forsyth-Grant had aggravated the incident.

He added: "Grant seemed to think he had some right to take over command of the boat and the crew. His attitude annoyed me and I probably did use abusive language."

Thomson told the court he asked the boarding party to leave his boat.

He told them they were trespassing.

He agreed that at one stage he had probably threatened to throw Grant overboard.

The jury found the skipper guilty of carrying off the boarding party—but recommended leniency "because of Grant's action which had agitated the situation."

Sheriff Principal Robert Taylor imposed a fine of £50 on this charge, saying that he accepted their recommendation.

He imposed a fine of £2500 or a year's jail on the charge of destroying evidence.

119

The other drift netters were undeterred by this episode, and the headlines it obtained from the media, and within days the fleet was back in Lunan Bay. And this was after the close of the official salmon season there.

I watched the fleet fishing with a telescope from Boddin Point, and asked Johnstons to scramble the speedboat and alert the police and meet me with the redoubtable Alec Coull and Donald MacIntyre, but Police Sergeant Bowshire and Constable Burnett of Arbroath declined to join on the counter-offensive, and stated they would witness proceedings from the sand dunes!

The boat was launched from the sands with the most helpful assistance of Angus Smart, the local net fishing foreman, and *Trafalgar* raced ahead to duel with the *Spitfire of Dunbar*, (skipper, RM Davies). *Spitfire* saw us coming, and made off seawards. We started to lift the inshore end of the drift net, and were quite well along the net with 22 salmon inboard when we observed *Spitfire* coming in to attack. We cut the drift net and got clear to manoeuvre. Of course we had treble the speed of the *Spitfire* and easily avoided the attempt to ram us, or the threat to do so! I ordered *Spitfire* to sail for Montrose under arrest, but the skipper refused, and set sail for the Forth.

When we returned ashore, the police took note of our story and said they would take possession of the net and salmon. Being very dubious if the police had a satisfactory remit of proceedings to be taken, I asked if we could all meet in Montrose that evening with the Arbroath Fishery Officer and thrash out what charges should be laid. Having

The Second Drift War

Police confiscating nets: second Drift Net War.

obtained *Spitfire*'s name and number, I requested the skipper be arrested and charged on arrival in Dunbar.

The authorities made the most disgraceful bungle of this case. Although a meeting was held at Montrose within hours of the incident which police, fishery officers and solicitors attended, and where a clear cut situation report on this incident was made, the Fiscal at Arbroath failed to issue the appropriate papers, and eventually time ran out and a criminal prosecution was thus time barred.

Not to be put off by this I consulted Frank Lefevre, the top solicitor of Aberdeen well known for his prowess in many major civil cases. Frank mastered the intricacies of the case very quickly, and a civil prosecution was instigated, finally presented by Counsel, Dr Taylor, QC (later Sheriff Principal).

Skipper and crew of the *Spitfire* were found guilty of this offence and interdict and other penalties enacted against them. It showed up the gross incompetence of those authorities involved in the case – the police, the fishery officer, St Andrews House and the Fiscal's department. Frank Lefevre added another feather to his cap in establishing the first and only civil case of marine salmon poaching ever to be privately instigated in Scottish history!

The drift net fleet now thought Lunan Bay was getting too hot and they started smaller raids off the North Kincardineshire coast. On one occasion we launched *Trafalgar* at Stonehaven in a heavy sea, and to the astonishment of the drift netter, we arrived alongside his nets, and began to lift the inshore end, watched by Grampian Police and the Superintendent of the River Dee Fishery Board. After inboarding some thirty salmon and part of the drift net, we observed the boat had fled the scene, but we had got her name and number and ordered her to Aberdeen but this was ignored. We handed the nets and salmon over the police and Dee Fishery Board at Newtonhill, and asked them to arrest and charge the skipper.

A few days later another drift netter appeared off Catterline, and we launched *Trafalgar* there in the presence of two police. Unfortunately, the motors of *Trafalgar* gave trouble, and we were unable to get the boat's name or number when she fled seawards to the Forth. We did recover salmon and part of the drift net.

The Second Drift War

I was determined not to be beaten by this, so I dashed by car to Montrose, having telephoned our office manager, Willie Johnston (ex-RAF wartime air crew), to get a private plane for me which I would join at Montrose Airfield, which belongs to Johnstons.

Within the hour I was winging away over the North Sea hunting down the drift netter. I soon spotted him, and we buzzed him several times before I got his number which I radioed to the police.

All these interceptions landed up in the sheriff courts. Thomson of the *Rosehaugh* was heavily fined in Arbroath, and narrowly missed a jail sentence. The case against the boat at Newtonhill was disgracefully bungled by the Procurator Fiscal at Stonehaven, who failed to charge under the correct

The war in the air: search and reconnaissance aircraft.

section, and the drift netters escaped with a derisory fine. When I remonstrated to the local press, the Fiscal rang me to say that if I persisted with my accusation, he would make things hot for me! I believe he would have done his damnedest, for he was a self-important little cock sparrow. I was relieved when he was transferred to another Sheriffdom shortly afterwards.

The pace was now getting too hot for me, and I asked for an assistant which was granted, and engaged Ian McCreadie Smith, a man who had served in Antarctic Survey ships and was then living in Montrose. Ian was a very different kettle of fish to Commander Brothers of the first Drift Net War. Admittedly he had suffered from a drink problem, but he was an excellent organizer and a good leader with an aggressive nature. Just what I wanted!

I gave Ian a pretty free hand to organize our counter-offensive which was getting quite as vicious as the first war. Johnstons were pretty well on their own this time, from Kinnaird Head to the Red Head of Angus, and self-financing. The River Tweed Fishery Board was also very active, and fighting there was even tougher, when a 'heavy mob' from Newcastle sank their patrol boat.

Ian set up his HQ in an office adjacent to mine, crewed by part-timers, with sea-going members and shore staff to handle transport radio and communications and even catering.

I still controlled the Intelligence Section, and to augment this, employed a very large and reputable firm of Edinburgh inquiry agents to infiltrate Port Seton and Dunbar, and I also controlled a large network of spies of my own.

The Second Drift War

These inquiry agents were most competent but expensive. They infiltrated one of their men as a crew member of a drift netter, whose reports were of enormous value. One fellow crew member suspected our man of being a fifth columnist and threw him off the quay into the harbour of a Forth port. This greatly enraged the other three members of this boat, who threw in the thrower! Shortly afterwards we withdrew our agent. He could have been killed.

A prawn processor of Port Seton was of great use to me. Every time the local fishing fleet went for salmon, they neglected the prawns, so his business suffered greatly. He kept ringing me personally to give me all sailing details and so forth. I never discovered who he was but he told me he would reveal himself in later years and would like to have a drink with me, so would a number of local fishermen who had once been my friends in minesweepers. Sadly, I am still waiting, and I sometimes wonder if a body found floating in the Forth could have been my secret agent.

Enough of the intelligence side of the operations. Suffice it to say that I felt obliged to put a public notice in the *Montrose Review* once an armistice had been declared.

Ian conducted the offensive extremely well, made many interceptions, and some arrests, one of the most notable of which was the *Dorothy Dee* of Montrose, skippered and owned by James Smart. He was fined £5,000. He resigned as coxwain of Montrose lifeboat as a result, and enlisted the help of Andrew Welsh, MP, who asked questions in the Commons. Relations with local RNLI were difficult. My two colleague Directors of Johnstons had a long association with the local lifeboat and held highest office, but in both Drift Net Wars I found the RNLI not so much neutral as hostile and I was glad that I never had to rely on them to be rescued. The local Secretary, Jack Smith of the *Montrose Review*, was one of my most ardent critics, and we conducted a vicious campaign of hate against each other in the *Review* and in other papers. When the war ended, we became friends again, as I did with Murray McBay, a drift netter exponent and lobster merchant of Johnshaven. (During the wars we entered the lobster market to sabotage his trade, which was a fair success. When the war ended, we gave up lobsters.)

Ian McCreadie Smith played a very major role in the second Drift Net War and was more responsible for winning it than any other individual. Sadly, I don't think his part was ever recognized in full except by the late Superintendent McIntyre of the South Esk Fishery Board and myself.

Ian was not popular with the police nor the local Fishery Officers, some of whom were in league with the law breakers as has been previously described.

At a successful prosecution in Arbroath Sheriff Court, the defence asked Ian if he was suggesting that a certain sergeant of police in the Lothian area had been alerting the drift netters with confidential information, to which Ian unwittingly replied in the affirmative, and too blandly. I was in court, and knew the sergeant in question was corrupt, but I kept many things like that to myself.

The Tayside police in Forfar — probably the federations boys at the back of it — threatened Ian very severely, and tired to make his life very difficult over this, and he got no support from those who had backed him. They were scared of the local police.

Ian was greatly hurt by this. Some time later, the Chief Inspector of Constabulary for Scotland, Mr David Gray, whom I had known for many years since he had been Chief Constable of Greenock, was my fishing guest at Morphie Dyke, and the second Drift Net War was obviously a talking point, although it had ended some time before. I told him in forthright terms of the disgraceful experience of Ian McCreadie Smith over this particular sergeant and was gratified to hear from the Chief Inspector that the offender had been transferred. I made certain that this conversation was well heard and witnessed.

Well, the second Drift Net War had drawn to a close by 1978. The inept Fisheries Division of Edinburgh came to life, as did their Fishery Cruisers, and began to enforce the Fisheries Laws for a change, virtually taking over from me and the splendid Tweed Board.

Unfortunately, Ian McCreadie Smith became redundant with this, and died not long afterwards, although I did my best to get him a job within the salmon protection industry.

So the troops were demobilized, and apart from showing the flag occasionally in Johnshaven and Auchmithie, the *Trafalgar* was mothballed and the operations room dismantled.

I would have liked to subscribe to a memorial and statue for Ian McCreadie Smith at the entrance to Montrose Harbour, but feelings still ran high, and like those erected to Stalin in his heyday, it might have been torn down or vandalized.

16

The Last Years

After the last few hectic years, 1979 came as a sort of anti-climax; I had divorced myself from all salmon advisory groups or they had divorced me! I had no time for all the lengthy meetings in Edinburgh with civil servants and other associated with salmon fisheries at government level, which I dismissed as a talking shop for professional windbags. I had seen enough of them in the National Farmers' Union. Admitted that someone with knowledge must be patient and attend those meeting and hopefully pressure-group the blundering mandamus of St Andrews House into some sort of knowledgeable legislation.

I was therefore free to devote my energies to sea-salmon fishings as practised for at least two centuries, but now much more mechanized, and with greatly reduced hours for all those seawise engaged.

The profits form commercial sea-salmon fishing were satisfactory, although we were reducing our sphere of operations. No longer did we fish north of Johnshaven. Over the period we held crown leases for North Kincardineshire, we had made an overall loss on these fishings. Nor had the sea fishings

The Last Years

between Gourdon and Stonehaven showed a profit for some years. The profitable areas were Montrose and Lunan Bay.

The company had very ample funds at its disposal after these years of profitability, and my colleagues through it wise to diversify, although against my own judgement.

We had failed to buy a large potato merchants company in the hope that it would provide winter work for seasonal salmon fishers. Apart from the fact that we failed to buy the company, the effort would have been wasted, because within years the business was much more mechanized and specialized, and had no requirement for extra winter labour.

The seasonal labour requirement was indeed a pressing need, for it we could not employ men all the year round; some would take permanent job elsewhere, and experienced men would be lost.

It was suggested that we should run a game and venison department, and that as a keen shooting man, I would be the right person to run it. Indeed I had considerable knowledge of the subject, as apart from game shooting and stalking all over the United Kingdom and the continent, I knew quite a few game dealers. They had an unfortunate knack of going bankrupt periodically, and then starting again.

A major game dealer in Scotland was George Mitchell of Letham in Angus. I had been dealing with his family for over 40 years, and while I took on my new task with misgivings, I knew I must involve someone with real knowledge of the merchanting business. So I suggested George, and he, my two colleagues and I started to negotiate.

Few people in Scotland had the knowledge or experience

of George. He was well known from Angus to Argyll, and from Fife to Sutherland. He was very popular with gamekeepers, and that was a massive advantage, for keepers controlled the selling of game and vermin rather than their employers, many of whom were absentee landlords. My two colleagues and I chartered a private aircraft and flew to Boston in Lincolnshire and visited the game factory of Butelaar, the largest in the UK. We also visited Van Dyjck's factory near Dusseldorf in Germany. He was a major importer of venison. However, the suggestion of a merger with George Mitchell was not a success, for various reasons, one being a clash of personalities and the other that George had a habit of being flush one year and broke the next! Notwithstanding, I counted him as my friend then, as I still do today!

So on my own I visited Frost Game, in Suffolk, the second largest game/venison dealer in the UK at the time, and Cecil Frost, the owner. I explored territory with him and we got on well, and I was flabbergasted when he suggested that his partner would like to join us, but he would continue on his own. He introduced me to Ron Scott, who had put quite a bit of money into Frost Game. I got on well with Ron, and, after a meeting in Montrose, with my colleagues, he joined us as Joint Managing Director of Johnstons Game Limited.

Without Ron Scott, Johnstons Game would never have got off the ground. He had the technical expertise in plucking and preparation that all three of us lacked. In no time we had a business running and producing game and rabbits for the consumer second to none, as I often proved going round the poultry and game sections of the largest London stores. However, the operations in Johnstons Game were all new recruits to Johnstons. They were women! So for a start it did not solve the labour problem.

In its day Johnstons Game became one of the largest names in oven-ready game in the UK and Ron Scott was an excellent Joint Managing Director, with a branch name of the Company in Suffolk. However, the ups and downs of the business that had caused Frost Game to go into liquidation, and George Mitchell the same way, hit the business badly, and it was eventually wound up and the staff dispersed. It was a big effort, sadly wasted, but there are some national trends which even quite a large company cannot withstand, including farm salmon, of which we shall hear more later.

My colleagues were not afraid of being venturesome. One project was for the storage of mud for North Sea oil drilling, so a grain warehouse with a big silo for storing the mud was bought. It never traded as such, and the silo was never filled and stands empty today.

After this project failed, the premises were let out for storage to a potato merchant, and it looked as if we could still get out of the impasse of this white elephant by selling it to him.

At our Annual General Meeting, the Chairman told the assembled shareholders that he had negotiated to sell the premises to a potato merchant and was congratulated by those present on getting rid of this unwanted warehouse. I staggered the meeting with a sour note. I told them the man in question had not the money nor the credit to buy the premises. I got some unfriendly looks, but within days the Chairman had to write the shareholders to confirm the deal was cancelled. The white elephant remained!

My two colleagues then decided to try the frozen food market, and a local entrepreneur Richard Robertson, whose wife had inherited a large profitable farm, was appointed as Managing Director of this project, to which Noël Smart gave the name of Esk Food; Esk being the name of the river from which the fortunes of Johnstons had derived.

My intuition and experience of Richard Robertson told me that a major investment in his company would be exceedingly risky for Johnstons. He had a different outlook to my colleagues; he was aggressive, self-confident and in my view, irresponsible. They were the opposite in spite of their friendship for him. Meetings were held to thrash out a joint participation, which I opposed. Within a short time Esk Food was virtually bust. Richard Robertson came back to Johnstons again, and had got Charles Alexander, the Aberdeen transport mogul, to back him. Again I opposed participation, and I got some very unkind looks for it and it was rightly held that I had been the stumbling block to an amicable partnership.

Within another short time Esk Food went really bust and Richard Robertson departed from the scene to the USA. Charlie Alexander later told me he had lost a lot of money.

The reader will rightly gather from the foregoing that I had a very negative attitude to diversification, and obviously had an effect on the attitude of my colleagues to me. Between them, they held the equity of the company and they decided, virtually on their own, to diversify into salmon fish-farming.

The Last Years

It was lucky they did not take my views into account. I would certainly have opposed it.

An experimental fish-farm was set up in Loch Sween, Argyll, in a very remote area, and was naturally very makeshift. My colleagues looked round for a suitable manager and found Dr Marshal Halliday, a young PhD in fisheries, and considered to be a rising star in the new profession. One thing I could agree, Marshal Halliday was an excellent choice, and the fish farm at Loch Sween progressed slowly from the experimental to the production stage.

Jonathan Stansfeld took the leading part in the initial stages of promoting this new venture, and he and Marshal Halliday explored the west coast of Scotland from the Clyde to Cape Wrath to find a large and more suitable site. They chose Badcall Bay, near Scourie in Sutherland.

Soon all the paraphernalia from Loch Sween was set up at Badcall, and Marshal Halliday ensconced as resident manager. It was one of the first large salmon-farms to be set up in Scotland and required an enormous injection of money to get it started. I had absolutely no say in the matter, in spite of being a Joint Managing Director, but of course, it was the company of my colleagues. I was already a minority shareholder.

In the early 1980s, the wild-salmon catching operation was fairly successful, but I faced a lot of grumbles from the sea-salmon fishers, who considered that they should be paid more for the profits they were making, and said that were it not for the money being poured into Badcall, their bonus would have been higher. There was a lot of truth in this.

I may well be considered a 'Dismal Desmond' but I had already seen the writing on the wall. There were clear signs that many of the stations Johnstons had operated from 1938–1980 were not profitable. All the profit was generated from Milton Ness to Boddin Point, about six miles as the crow flies, with Montrose in the centre.

Furthermore, there was a big decrease in profitability in the North Esk and South Esk river fishings which led me to believe that profitability in commercial salmon-catching was already doomed. A salmon on a fish-buyer's slab might fetch £25, but on the end of a rod it was worth £300. If anyone wanted to make a living out of salmon fishing it would be wiser to do it through angling rather than netting. This is becoming more and more obvious at the time I write this.

By 1984, the fish farms, which had expanded much from Badcall, took off and started returning a profit but it must be remembered that the investment had been enormous.

For about four years, while the profits from wild salmon became substantial losses, the farmed salmon showed a good return so that for three years the company was able to pay a dividend of some thirty per cent – a fairly good return for even a high-risk industry.

However, the writing was one the wall for fish farmers too. Salmon farms, like deer farms, were springing up like mushrooms from Dumfries to Shetland, and the same was happening in Norway with much better facilities. At Badcall, Dr Halliday was promoted to managing directorship and left there to take up office in Montrose. The discipline at Badcall, never easy to maintain but managed effectively by Marshal

Halliday, began to fall apart under his successors, who seemed to resign or face dismissal with regrettable frequency.

But I am running ahead. The troubles of salmon farming were just beginning when I left the company in 1986, and sadly I was glad to leave. There was nothing further I could do. The company had for years been very lucky to have the services of David Dundas, the salmon superintendent for many years up to 1984, and of Willie Johnston (no relation) the office manager for over 30 years. When these two retired within a couple of years of my own retiral, I could see little prospects of profitability in the more grandiose organization of office affairs in a troubled market.

By and large, commercial salmon-fishing in general, and Johnstons in particular, had done very well overall from 1947 to 1984 and then the decline started.

Although it might be said that at times my mind was on other things than the rigid organization of salmon netting at sea, I think that if it had gone into voluntary liquidation in 1986, the property assets would have exceeded the liabilities by more than £8,000,000 – not bad for a company with a share capital of £400,000. Most of this was achieved by property appreciation, such as Morphie and Gallery Angling, Montrose Airfield, R Pert's premises in Balmain Street and Brown's premises in River Street.

In 1986, fire insurance valuation on buildings alone came to £8,000,000, let alone the valuable angling of Morphie, Canterland and Gallery then worth at least £3,000,000 on their own. At the height of the property boom, with the rather grudging approval of my colleagues, I sold the one-acre net green at Bervie – just a tangle of bent grass on shingle – for £30,000! Today, I doubt if anyone would offer £1,000 for it. The would-be developers had gone mad.

From 1948–1986, I think it is likely that the profits from property appreciation would have exceeded all those from salmon fishing. It seems an appalling state of affairs, but I think it is a fact. While I think it ethically wrong to make such hugh profits out of property, one would be stupid to let other do it and be left out in the cold because of one's conscience.

I am glad I left the company's service when I did, since when I have sold off my shares and, other than my pension, have no connection whatsoever.

The company was good to me in many ways. Paying me throughout the war, they gave me a very kind send-off when I left. I enjoyed my time with them, in spite of the very different points of view between me and my colleagues. For me, 1986 was the end of an era. I would sooner remember the past than the future.

Index

Adams,	David, Foreman Salmon Fisher	25
Arbuthnott & Son,	Boatbuilders	60
Bairn's Pride.,	MFV	94
Bell,	Police Constable	119
Billingsgate Market		31
Blues,	Tom, Salmon Fisher, Bon Viveur	77
Bowshire,	Police Sgt. (Later Supt.)	120
Brothers,	Lieut. Cdr. RN. (Retd.)	97, 100
Burnett,	Major General Sir James	104
Burnett,	Police Constable	120
Burnett,	Roger, Landowner's son	103
Canterland Fishings		35
Christie,	Duncan, Foreman Carpenter	19, 39, 73
Clark,	George, Foreman Salmon Fisher	35
Clark,	John, Foreman Salmon Fisher	31
Coull,	Alec, Foreman Motor Mechanic	117
Coull,	John, Supt. of Salmon Fishings	17, 31, 48, 89
Craigo Fishing,	Station	34
Crathes Castle		36

Crowe,	Jim, Mussel Foreman,	40
Crowe,	Frank, Mussel Foreman	42
Dalhousie,	Earl of	112
Davies,	R.M., Fishing Boat Skipper	120
Dorothy Dee,	MFV	125
Farnham Angling Club		78
Fishery Board for Scotland		13
Forsyth-Grant,	Osbert Clare, Explorer	40
Foster,	Major D., Landowner	107
Frost,	Cecil, Game Dealer	130
George V,	Silver Jubilee	8
Gilbert,	Bill	109
Gray,	David, CBE. QPM, Chief Inspector of Constabulary for Scotland	127
Halliday,	Dr. Marshall, Pisciculturist	133
Harrington,	James, Engineering Tycoon & Angler	109
Harvey,	William	95
Henderson,	Petty Officer George	53
Johnston,	J. Noel, Company Director & Benefactor	73
Johnston,	Willie, Office Manager	123
Johnston,	Provost W. Douglas, OBE	17, 20, 36, 37, 53, 59, 62
Kelly,	Foreman Mechanic	19
Kenn,	John, Salmon Skipper	78
Kola River		58

Index

Lefevre,	Frank, Prominent Aberdeen Solicitor	121
Loddon,	River	7
McBay,	Craigie	41
McBay,	Dick	95
McBay,	Murray, Lobster Merchant	126
McBay,	Wattie	41
McCreadie Smith, Ian		124, 126, 127
MacFarlane,	P.R.C., Deputy later Chief Inspector of Salmon Fisheries	12, 48
Macintyre,	Supt. Donald	94, 117, 118, 119
Mackie,	Alec, Salmon Boat Skipper	78
Mackie,	D. D., Foreman Salmon Fisher	63
Mackis,	Alec, Salmon Boat Skipper	78
MacLeay,	H. M. J. S. (Lord Muirshiel, Secretary of State for Scotland)	100
Maiden,	Harry & Co. Montrose Blacksmiths	76
Mearns,	Willie (Codling), Fisherman	45, 46, 47, 57, 66
Menzies,	W. J. M. CBE, Inspector of Salmon Fisheries	12, 13, 37
Miller,	Supt. Tay Fisheries Board	94
Milne,	Roland, Foreman Salmon Fisher	48, 106
Mitchell,	George, Game Dealer	129
Morphie Dyke		30, 32, 34
Morrison Brothers,	MFV Owner Skippers	99
Nelson College		10, 13, 14, 15
Northesk, River		21
Oor Lass,	MFV	91, 92

Paton,	"Coullie", Gourdon Fisherman & Chief Petty Officer RNR	53
Pert,	David, Ferryden Fisherman	41
Pittendreich,	George	2
Pondage Pool		37
Powell,	Police Constable	119
Powrie Clan,	Salmon Tacksmen	74
Rawlins,	John, (Surgeon Vice Admiral Sir J.)	7
Renny-Tailyour,	Colonel	9
Rosehaugh,	MFV	117
Ryan,	Colonel Michael, Chief Ex. Tweed River Board	100
Salmon,	John (Jock), Farmer	68
Scott,	Ron, Game Dealer	130
Scott Robinson,	Sheriff Stanley MBE	92
Shewan,	Leslie, Police Inspector	46
Sierra Leone		58
Silver Fern,	MFV	94
Smart,	Angus, Foreman Salmon Fisher	70
Smart,	G. C. J., Company Director	17, 61, 67, 82
Smart,	G. N. J., Company Director	117
Smart,	James, MFV Skipper	125
Smith,	Jack D., Journalist & MFV Owner	126
Smythe,	Andrew, Provost of Forfar	81
Soutar,	Alastair, Salmon Fisher & Chief P.O.	53
Soutar,	David, Foreman Mason/Bricklayer	76
Southesk, River		10, 26
Souvenir,	Converted MFV Patrol Boat	96, 98
Spitfire,	MFV	120
Stansfeld,	Captain J. de B.M.C.	17, 34, 51, 53, 61
Stansfeld,	J. R. W., Company Director	89

Index

St. Andrews House		12
Stewart,	James, Salmon Skipper	44, 54
Stewart,	John, Salmon Skipper	44
Swankie,	MFV Skipper	95
Taylor,	Dr. Q. C., Sheriff Principal	122
Thomson,	W. F. Skipper MFV "Rosehaugh"	117
Thornton,	Cdr. Mark DSO DSC	56
Torrie,	David, Superintendent of Salmon Fishings	49
Trafalgar,	High Speed Patrol Boat	117, 127
Ulcerative Dermal Necrosis		71, 79
Valentine,	Charles, Slater and Angler	86, 106, 107
Webster,	Neil, Salmon Tractor Driver	65
Wellington College		5, 6, 10
Welsh,	Andrew, M.P.	125
Whitewater River		9
Winder,	Peter, Ghillie	111
Woodroffe,	Col. Jack	112
Wright,	Isaac, River Bailiff Supt	68, 85, 89
Wyllie,	Harry, Salmon Skipper	76